Praise for *Imagine That*

"*If you want to grow in your understanding of what it means to be an artist for Christ, if you want a working theology of the arts, or if you want to learn what God says about the arts (and artists), read this book! Manuel Luz speaks authoritatively from God's Word and convincingly from his many years of experience. Throughout the book, you will laugh at some of his personal anecdotes, be stirred by his ideas, and be motivated by his passion. But more importantly, you will be drawn closer to Christ.* "

Rory Noland, author, director of Heart of the Artist Ministries

"*Manuel Luz has made a good and helpful contribution to the present-day conversation surrounding the arts and Christian faith. Discover for yourself the unique calling of those privileged to imagination for Jesus and His kingdom coming. You'll be enriched and inspired.*"

Charlie Peacock, co-director Art House America and
author of *New Way To Be Human*

"*In this much needed work, Manuel Luz paints for us a theology of art that is as stimulating as it is biblical. Forged from the pen of an artist, this book provides fresh insights into how a postmodern generation can engage the God who creates and re-creates.*"

Christian George, author of *Sex, Sushi & Salvation: Thoughts on Intimacy, Community & Eternity* and *Godology: Because Knowing God Changes Everything*

"*I always think of Manuel Luz as the rocket scientist who became a worship arts leader. This book is written out of the trenches of Manuel's discoveries as an artist, pastor, and worship leader who serving the local church. I deeply appreci*

and believe it will serve as a tremendous tool for any Christian artist looking for guidance from someone who has wrestled with the Scriptures, theological truth, and the practical everyday challenges of unleashing artistic gifts in the kingdom of God."

Nancy Beach, Champion for the Arts,
Willow Creek Association, and author of *An Hour on Sunday: Creating Moments of Transformation and Wonder*

"Manuel Luz and I have recorded together, prayed together, cried together, and ministered together in America and beyond over the last twenty years. In Imagine That he has written what amounts to a theology of the Christian arts. I can't think of anyone more practically qualified to write about this subject; he has thought about it and he has lived it. If you're looking for your place as a Christian artist, you will surely find trustworthy pathway markers for your journey in this book. Imagine that!"

Bob Kilpatrick, songwriter/producer, author, and speaker

MANUEL LUZ

Discovering Your Unique Role
as a **Christian Artist**

IMAGINE
THAT

MOODY PUBLISHERS

CHICAGO

All Scripture quotations, unless otherwise indicated, are taken from the *Holy Bible, New International Version*®. NIV®. Copyright © 1973, 1978, 1984 by International Bible Society. Used by permission of Zondervan. All rights reserved.

Scripture quotations marked NASB are taken from the *New American Standard Bible*®, Copyright © 1960, 1962, 1963, 1968, 1971, 1972, 1973, 1975, 1977, 1995 by The Lockman Foundation. Used by permission. (www.Lockman.org)

Scripture quotations marked NLT are taken from the *Holy Bible, New Living Translation*, copyright © 1996, 2004. Used by permission of Tyndale House Publishers, Inc., Wheaton, Illinois 60189, U.S.A. All rights reserved.

Scripture quotations marked THE MESSAGE are from *The Message*, copyright © by Eugene H. Peterson 1993, 1994, 1995. Used by permission of NavPress Publishing Group.

All websites listed herein are accurate at the time of publication but may change in the future or cease to exist. The listing of website references and resources does not imply publisher endorsement of the site's entire contents. Groups, corporations, and organizations are listed for informational purposes, and listing does not imply publisher endorsement of their activities.

Editor: Elizabeth Newenhuyse
Interior Design: Smartt Guys
Cover Design: Dog Eared Design
Cover Image: iStockPhoto

Library of Congress Cataloging-in-Publication Data

Luz, Manuel.
    Imagine that : discovering your unique role as a Christian artist / Manuel Luz.
        p. cm.
    Includes bibliographical references.
    ISBN 978-0-8024-2450-1
    1. Christianity and art. 2. Artists—Religious life. I. Title.
BR115.A8L89 2009
261.5'7—dc22

                                            2009006868

We hope you enjoy this book from Moody Publishers. Our goal is to provide high-quality, thought-provoking books and products that connect truth to your real needs and challenges. For more information on other books and products written and produced from a biblical perspective, go to www.moodypublishers.com or write to:

Moody Publishers
820 N. LaSalle Boulevard
Chicago, IL 60610

1 3 5 7 9 10 8 6 4 2

Printed in the United States of America

Dedicated to the hundreds of artists with whom
I have had the privilege of sharing the creative experience.
And a special thanks to my loving wife
for supporting the artist that is me.

CONTENTS

FOREWORD

I often find myself speaking with people who are at the end of their resources, facing situations in life where their old ways of surviving and fixing things just aren't working. They are hungering for a fresh way to experience the world, and God, and themselves, because the ruts of their inner world have them stuck and stagnant. In these situations I often find myself asking people, "What are you doing to create? Where are you stirring up the artistic impulse?"

And that impulse could be writing, music, poetry, drawing, pottery, sculpture, painting, photography; it could be cooking, gardening, knitting, working in graphic arts, scrapbooking. The examples could go on and on. Since we've been made in the image of our Creator God, I believe there is something within the heart of every human being that not only wants to create, but *needs* to create. In our increasingly consumer- and spectator-oriented culture, there is a great need in all of us to bring something beautiful into being that didn't exist before.

My good friend Manuel Luz has brought something beautiful into existence with this book, and I am thrilled you are reading it. I have known Manuel for over twenty years and have worked with him in the trenches of church life for most of that time. Manuel is not a theorist in this area of creativity and the arts. He is a practitioner. This book is the result of a couple of decades of hard work, careful thinking, and diligent and inspired art-making. On top of all this, and perhaps most importantly, Manuel brings a pastoral heart to this topic. I have seen him work with artists of greater and lesser gifting. The fascinating thing is that Manuel celebrates and enjoys both to the same degree. He really believes one of the main messages of this book: When we create, we declare the beauty and glory of God — who Himself loves to create — and are transformed in the process.

I did a quick bit of estimating and discovered that over the past twenty years, Manuel and I have been involved in around 3,500 worship services together. I get tired just typing those words. Each one of the services required a creative meeting to plan for it. Then, of course, there were the rehearsals. Along with all the music, there were often dramas, reader's theater, multimedia presentations, dance, painting, graphic art, etc. After it was all said and done, I would find myself wanting to sit in front of the television and watch a soccer game from Argentina, but Manuel kept making art. After work hours he would stay up late creating music, putting albums together, blogging about art-making, and writing this book. He told me once, "Kent, all the worship services we put together are fun, but they kind of make me feel like a horse in a corral. To stay fresh about my art, I have to get out into some open spaces and just create."

It is my prayer that this book will send all who read it out into the open spaces to make art in order to reflect the beautiful and creative nature of God.

Kent Carlson
Co-Senior Pastor
Oak Hills Church
Folsom, California

INTRODUCTION

It was the mid-eighties—the era of big hair, Levi's 501 jeans with Converse high-tops, and girls who just wanted to have fun—and I was in a local cover band called Fixation.

Actually, the band was really just a duo, although we would add a drummer or bass player, depending on the amount of money we were paid. My partner, Bob, sang and played electric guitar, and I filled out the sound with vocals, right-handed keyboards, left-handed key bass, and a drum machine triggered with my left foot. Armed with a playlist that included Motown, trash rock, oldies, and post-disco, we played dive bars all across northern California, from Placerville to Stockton to Vacaville. My favorite compliment: "Dude! You sound just like a band!"

Fixation was one of many musical expressions along the adventure of my life, one short on highlights but long on memories. I did it for a number of reasons. For one, I felt that I needed the experience of playing these hard four-hour sets. Also, I used the money to buy more music equipment. And finally, in a weird kind of way, I actually liked it.

We were booked one weekend at the Woodlake Inn, a huge venue with an expansive dance floor and a wide bar that stretched along the back of the room. It was a convention hotel, with extensive stage lighting, a high stage, and the obligatory disco ball hanging from the ceiling, so our duo was swallowed up by the room. It didn't really matter though, because no one was there. By contract, we began playing our first set at 9:00 p.m. to about a hundred empty chairs and stools, one bartender, and two waitresses. It was going to be a *long* night.

During the first break (and the first of many ginger ales), the double doors suddenly flung open, and about a hundred people floated in. *Finally! A crowd!* we thought to ourselves, as a convention group had apparently let out for the evening. We hustled back onstage and began playing our best dance stuff: Huey Lewis, flat out. And as we finished the song with a big trash can ending, the crowd responded—with deafening silence.

Beads of sweat began to form on our foreheads. Okay, maybe they weren't Huey fans. So we quickly launched into an exaggerated version of "Caribbean Queen." If there were one dance chromosome in the entire room, Billy Ocean would certainly summon these latent genes to the hardwood. But despite the pounding kick drum and driving bass (and the disco ball), the floor remained empty. After the song ended, I could almost swear I heard crickets.

Everyone likes the blues, Bob reasoned, so we launched into a soulful B. B. King—inspired version of "Stormy Monday." And after that was over—yes, those were *definitely* crickets outside. I checked my watch and did the mental calculation: *Okay, you can do this. Only 153 more minutes and it will all be over.*

In desperation, we played a slow ballad, I can't remember what—something by Hall and Oates maybe. And between verses, I squinted to see beyond the blinding stage lights. What I saw almost stopped me in mid-song. There, across the tables, were a hundred people—

laughing, drinking, unwinding—and silently gesturing to one another in sign language.

Squinting beyond the stage lights to see those many people speaking to one another with their hands, it became obvious that I didn't really understand who my audience was. And without knowing your audience, you can't truly know what makes their hearts beat fast, what puts smiles on their faces, what makes them dance. This is true for our horizontal audience, and it is equally true of our vertical audience as well, our Audience of One.

This book was born, in part, out of a desire to understand myself. One day, after being a creative arts pastor for over fourteen years, I suddenly came to the realization that I had no real theology of art. That is, I didn't have any systematic understanding of God as it related to art and the artist. More personally, I had no practical understanding of God as it related to the artist that is me. I had some ideas, things I had learned and picked up over the years, but I really had no *theology* upon which I could understand myself as an artist, or how God perceives and receives my art, or the nature of God as an Artist, or even my role as a creative arts pastor. In a real sense, I realized that my understanding of my art as it related to my faith was insufficient, incongruent, incomplete. And if that is the case, then do I really know what I'm doing with my life?

This is not necessarily something to brag about.

In greater degree, this book emerged from a desire to know God's heart. I want to know God, in deeper and profound and intimate ways. And as an artist, I want to understand with greater clarity God's calling upon me and His relationship with me. I want to be motivated by a heart that follows His heart, to love what He loves, to sense His leadings, to be an artist that follows the Artist.

So this book is a personal journey of sorts, to form a working theology of art. I purposed my devotional reading and pondering and praying to the task. I kept a journal of my thoughts. And I kept my eyes and ears open to any God sightings. And this is what I came up with.

Now, my disclaimers: The word *theology* often implies something grandiose, academic, profound. But this theology of art isn't that ambitious. My intent was to make it practical and personal, not clinical and theoretical, in the style of a master's thesis. I just wanted to make it real to my life. My theology is simply what I believe of God. Also, theology might imply that somehow it's all been figured out, as if our understanding of God can be reduced to a formula or a compendium. But in its essence, a theology is still about a relationship with the living Triune God, and I have a great respect for the mystery of this relationship, and how un-formulaic relationships are.

Faith is a journey. And the journey is as much the point as the destination. So this is simply my understanding of it all so far. Above all, it has been an adventure, in my faith and in my art.

And our nightmare gig playing for the convention of hearing-challenged people? They approached us between sets and told us to turn it up. Way, way up. They couldn't hear the music, but when we played louder, they could feel it. And after we turned up the decibels, they spent the last two sets dancing to every single song we played.

Imagine that.

Chapter 1

GOD
the ARTIST

MADE IN HIS IMAGE

"Daddy, draw me a horse."

So begins a typical scene in my home. One of my twin daughters, Rachel or Paige, will appear beside me with a colored marker pen and a sheet of paper, and ask me to become Artist Daddy. Most of the time, it's not difficult. Horses, stars, dogs, cats, and flowers are typical requests from six-year-old girls, and they measure the quality of my work not by its realism, but by whether or not the characters are smiling. In a former life, I was a cartoonist for my college newspaper. So I accept the challenge. I take the pen from her delicate fingers, smooth out her crumpled paper, and draw.

The result is part caricature, part cave drawing, but she is delighted nonetheless. "Thanks, Daddy," she will offer politely. And then she will muse, "Her name is . . . um . . . Buttercup." And then she will color it and add green grass, a yellow sun in the corner, and eyelashes (because this is how little girls distinguish girl horsies from boy horsies).

This, to me, is a picture of the first chapter of Genesis. God the Father is also God the Creator. It is not just what He does; it is more precisely who He is. It is not a gig for Him; it is inherent in His very nature. And because He is the Creator, the Artist God, He must stretch the canvas of infinite emptiness around Him, and wish for more. Then, from the eternal imagination that is His nature, He begins to paint: galaxies, nebulae, capacious, dynamic kaleidoscopes of light and energy and mass, churning and coagulating at His fingertips. Mass yields to gravity, atoms become molecules, stars begin their intricate dance. Cosmos comes from chaos. And by His very will, the Artist God paints the universe we know and understand and live in.

WE CREATE BECAUSE WE ARE MADE IN THE IMAGE OF THE CREATOR. WE SIMPLY CANNOT HELP IT.

Then He stands back. He puts down His palette, cleans His brush, examines the easel. He smells the wet acrylic, feels the interplay of colors on the canvas. He takes it all in, and then He slowly smiles. And then He calls it "good."

But He is not done yet. He calls on His creation, that which is humanity, that which is privileged to experience the wonder of it all, and invites him to participate in this creation. Abba God calls Adam to His side, and then gives him a job to do: to name the animals. And in so doing, He calls us to be creative ourselves. The created becomes creator, the art becomes artist. We are invited into the mystery of His inborn aesthetic.

Genesis says that we are made in His image. This is more profound than we know. We are made with intellects, with the amazing capacity to understand and ponder and offer explanations about the world around us. We have sentience, the awareness of our own being and a consciousness of the universe. We have the ability to build machines, create cities, form entire civilizations, and then destroy them. We can philosophize, moralize, theorize, and know good and evil.

And we are made not just as physical beings, but as spiritual beings as well. We are made with a capacity to love as He loved. To have free will, as He has free will. To choose the course of our own lives. And also, to create as He creates. To express ourselves in artistic and imaginative ways. In short, we are artists because He is an artist.

Thus, as artists, we are endowed with both the ability and the desire to create, and the ability to derive pleasure from it. We create because we are made in the image of the Creator. We simply cannot help it. This is why Michelangelo painted the Sistine Chapel. This is why Homer told his stories. This is why Shakespeare penned his dramas. This is why David played the ten-string lyre. This is why children draw and play-act and imagine.

That is who we are: artists. Children of the Creator. We grasp at sunsets and attempt to paint them. We hear the sound of the ocean and compose sonnets in its honor. We see the autumn swans dance, and we dance. And we draw horses named Buttercup.

DISCOVERING THE PASSION

When I was a little boy, more than anything else in the world, I wanted to be a concert pianist. Of course, more than anything else in the world, I wanted to be a police officer and an astronaut and Spider-Man. Still, my mind was consumed in a fascination for classical music. Chopin, Mozart, Beethoven, and Schroeder were my idols. Liberace was my antichrist. And by the age of thirteen, Bach had become my hero.

My parents tell me that I first began to take lessons when I was almost five. My first piano teacher was a little old prunelike lady named Mrs. Branoni. I would extrapolate ten-second minuets like "Putt Putt the Speed Boat" for her as we sat perched on the piano bench, my legs dangling, her toes keeping time. Occasionally, she would nod off, only to be awakened when I asked her a question. And if I played well, she would stick a silver or gold star on the page. I liked that a lot.

From that time until I was fourteen, I banged away on an over-sized, out-of-tune mahogany upright, putt-putting through a dozen piano teachers along the way. I loved that piano, loved the sound that it made, loved the control I had of it, loved the security of being behind it. In good ways and in bad, it became a part of my identity.

I played my piano noncommittally, never putting a lot of thought or effort into it, never needing to. From the time I can remember, I'd always had this magical ability to play almost anything on the piano that I could hum. Seriously, I thought I had composed "Heart and Soul" when I was six.

Then came Professor Krauss. Professor Krauss was a stocky German with square features and big, burly hands that played with mesmerizing authority and exactitude. He was a passionate man, passionate about this thing called music. And the passion was contagious.

Twice a month, he drove his Mercedes diesel from Carmel Valley to my home on the poor side of Salinas to teach this short, fat, twelve-year-old Filipino kid with glasses. He challenged me, opened my mind, opened my heart. There was something inside me that awoke during that time, something that helped me transcend the ordinariness of my life. Without knowing it, Professor Krauss changed my life.

One day, he brought me a skinny yellow book filled with *lots* and *lots* of notes. They were called "Inventions" and they were written by a guy named Johann, which I thought was oddly cool. Bach was a different kind of guy. There was something about him, not just the precision of his work, but the emotion that lay within it. It was only later that I discovered that the passion of his music came from his faith. Johann Sebastian Bach—artist, composer, keyboard innovator, definer of his genre—was first and foremost a worshiper of the Living God. Everything he did was for God's honor, and not his own: "The aim and final end of all music should be none other than the glory of God and the refreshment of the soul." One day I hope to meet him in heaven. Maybe take a lesson or two.

Under the tutelage of Professor Krauss, I learned discipline and control, dexterity and nuance. I learned the craft. And I caught the passion. Two years later, he had to leave, but not without a last word: "Keep pragtizing your finger egzercises, yah? Like dis, yah?" And I do. To this day.

That was three decades ago. Since then, I have moved on from my puppy-dog love affair with classical music. There was rock and roll—naive and exciting like a teenage crush—which my brothers and I discovered on the AM band of the living room stereo. Then came jazz—like the bad girl who flirts with you when you're on a date—and I learned that the rules of music were made to be broken. I have played pop, soul, country, blues, Dixieland, big band, reggae, R&B, church music, smooth jazz, and trash rock and roll. I've played in cover bands, coffeehouse groups, marching bands, symphonic bands, fusion bands, and garage bands. And whatever the style, the passion remains.

I have come to realize that this passion is more than just a hobby. I believe it was put inside of me from the moment I was born. It was in me when I climbed on a piano bench for the first time. It was in me when I took clarinet lessons. It was in me when I played my first solo, wrote my first song, recorded my first demo, formed my first band, produced my first album, first sang a song in the shower. It is in me today. Because I don't just *play* music; I am a musician. I don't *do* art; I am an artist. More than just what I do, it is who I am. That is who God made me to be.

"For you created my inmost being; you knit me together in my mother's womb. . . . My frame was not hidden from you when I was made in the secret place. When I was woven together in the depths of the earth, your eyes saw my unformed body. All the days ordained for me were written in your book before one of them came to be" (Psalm 139:13, 15–16).

This is the way for everyone, I believe. We are all artists, fashioned by the Artist, to create, reveal, and interpret the world. Some of us have more skill or talent or ability than others. But all of us have this innate artistic predisposition within us, placed there by the Creator. Some of us have just never found the passion. And that is a shame.

I didn't become a cop. I didn't work for NASA. I wasn't bitten by a radioactive spider. But I do believe that God made me with a passion for music. And I must be true to that.

The Artist Incarnate

Someone asked me once if Jesus Christ had been an artist. "Good question," I replied.

We talked about the vocation of His stepfather, Joseph of Nazareth, who was not only "a righteous man" (Matthew 1:19), but also a carpenter, a craftsman of wood. The carpenter, rather than today's modern notion of the carpenter as house builder, was more so a craftsman, a skilled artisan. Not so much a hammerer of nails, but more a shaper of wood. It was an artistic craft that took many years of training to master.

We talked about how it is the Jewish custom (as in many premodern cultures) to pass on one's skills to the sons, and how the natural implications of that custom would have impacted this firstborn son. It would have been the responsibility of Joseph to pass on the skills of the trade to Jesus, in order that his son would have a vocation and a future. So although nothing is said of Joseph's relationship with his stepson, one would assume that Jesus knew the craft from an early age and that it was the vocational context upon which He saw life.

We talked about a wonderful quote I read once in Madeleine L'Engle's book *Walking on Water*, which read: "Jesus was not a theologian. He was God who told stories."[1] That is not to say that Jesus was not wise nor learned, as evidenced in the account of Luke, for he says of the twelve-year-old Jesus in the temple, "Everyone who heard him was amazed at his understanding and his answers" (Luke 2:47). But He was not a theoretician, one who systematizes and extrapolates and publishes. Instead, He told parables, Truth so practical and real and profound that it confounded the Pharisees and delighted the crowds and cut to the very essence of being.

The Lost Coin. The Prodigal Son. The House on the Sand. The Mustard Seed. The Sower. The Pearl of Great Price. The Plank in Your Eye. The Lilies of the Field. The Lost Sheep. The Bread Which Was His Body. The Wine Which Was His Blood.

Jesus was speaking of unfathomable mysteries. And the words we have invented to unravel these mysteries—words like propitiation, incarnation, atonement, ecclesiology, grace—are simply too small and inadequate to fully describe and explain the truth. And maybe our brains are just a little too small to fully understand them anyway. So when He spoke, it was necessary to use the *art* of words—metaphors and similes and parables—to more adequately express the depth of truth that is the cosmic drama. As if this mortal life we live were simply a metaphor for some larger eternal life He invites us to.

Jesus was a master of the parable, the simile, the metaphor. He spoke Truth wrapped in the art of storytelling. The eternal Word, speaking the Truth of the Word, with the art of words.

And we talked about John's poetic extension of Genesis 1, a revelation of the person of Jesus, which is found in his first chapter: "In the beginning was the Word, and the Word was with God, and the Word was God. He was with God in the beginning. Through him all things were made; without him nothing was made that has been made" (John 1:1–3; see also Colossians 1:15–17 and 1 Corinthians 8:6). Jesus is eternal, one in essence with the Eternal Father and Eternal Spirit. Jesus was not only present in the act of creation, but the act of creation happened *through Him*.

> BEING AN ARTIST IS NOT JUST ABOUT WHAT YOU DO, BUT ALSO HOW YOU LIVE YOUR LIFE.

This is so deep as to be astounding. The creative muse of the Trinity mysteriously and inexplicably poured through the Person of the pre-incarnate Son. Was it Jesus who said, "The sun shall be yellow" and "the sky shall be blue"? Did He give peanut butter its taste, and the hummingbird its flight? Was He the inventor of the dimensions, of length and breadth and height and time? Was He the creator of the sun and moon and planets, and the choreographer of their cosmic spirographic dance?

And finally, He was God in the flesh. He was the Incarnation, the fleshing out of Deity. He was the human personification and embodiment of God Himself. In the act of incarnation, through birth and life and death and resurrection, He indwelled that which He Himself created. So He was the Artist who was literally present within His Art.

Was Jesus an Artist? I believe He was. But not only by vocation. Maybe by Inspiration. He lived His entire life—His relationships, His ministry, His calling—as an art. He lived and loved deeply and with passion. He lived from the heart. I'd like to believe that He was an artist, manifesting this descriptor physically, emotionally, and spiritually. Because being an artist is not just about what you do, but also how you live your life.

LEARNING TO LIVE IN THE MYSTERY

One of the Christmastime traditions my wife and I established with our children when they were young was looking at the Christmas lights around our community. Bundled up under blankets in our minivan (the twenty-first-century version of the horse-drawn sleigh), the entire family would go driving down one street and up another, looking at all the decorated houses in our neighborhood.

And people would go all out. Life-sized reindeer. Nativity scenes. Santas coming down chimneys. Snowmen with top hats and pipes. Candy canes lining people's driveways. And lights. Lots and lots of lights. The more the lights, the more we'd "ooh" and "aah." Then we'd drive back to our house and have hot cocoa.

> KIDS DON'T LOOK UP AT THE CLOUDS ANYMORE AND IMAGINE BUNNIES AND MINNOWS.

It was in their third Christmas that my twins, Rachel and Paige, were old enough to really appreciate the event. And that they did. Through their little three-year-old eyes, our neighborhood was a magical and amazing place. Every house glowed like fresh-baked gingerbread. Trees glistened like the moonlight on fresh-fallen snow. And everywhere there were lights, Rachel and Paige announced excitedly, "Ommagosh, it's bootiful."

It was extremely entertaining listening to them. They must have said it two hundred times. And every time they made this startling declaration, they really, really meant it. "Ommagosh, it's bootiful." "Ommagosh, it's bootiful." "Ommagosh! It's bootiful!!!" I never got tired of hearing them say it. It was as if each street was a new adventure in awe and wonder.

I think we've forgotten what real awe is. Our high-tech, computer-generated, virtual-reality, angst-ridden, dysfunctional world has taken much of the mystery and wonder out of life. Kids don't look up at the clouds anymore and imagine bunnies and minnows; after all, they studied precipitation in third grade. They don't take much time imagining dinosaurs; there are any number of movies out there that have imagined them for us already. Science—which teaches theory as fact and conjecture as theory—has erased all of the mysteries. Just ask any kid and he'll tell you: the very mysteries of the universe are carefully and regularly explained in half-hour segments on the Discovery Channel.

My sons aren't nearly as impressed by the sight of a rainbow as I used to be when I was their age. Or as I am still.

Things I used to be in awe of when I was a little kid: Purple mountains. Big telescopes. Airplanes. Thunder. Pretty girls. Lighthouses. Big bass drums. Red fire trucks. Stoplights. Crossword puzzles. Our first color television. Walking on the moon. Snow. The doctor's office. Policemen. Sousaphones. The pyramids. Rockets. Big cities. The redwoods. The stars on a cloudless night sky.

Things I used to think were mysterious: The Teacher's Lounge. Solar eclipses. Driving a car. The ocean. The adult section of the public library. Sharks. My big brother's View Master slide viewer. Electricity. Slide rules. Dinosaurs. Ships in bottles. Car engines.

Make up your own list. Then ask your child to make up one. You'll see what I mean. There is a reason why the song "Twinkle, Twinkle, Little Star" is a toddler favorite. Because wrapped up in six short lines is the awe and wonder of the universe.

I grew up in the Roman Catholic Church. And although I am a little more aligned with evangelicalism now, I have great respect for and warm recollections of my Catholic heritage. There was something about being in my church as a child. Sitting in the pew, being painted by the colored beams of light streaming through the stained glass.

Watching the rows of lit candles dance. Kneeling on the cold white marble as I took Communion, the kinesthetic symbolism of that white wafer melting on my tongue. These were powerful moments for me as a child, moments when I understood God in a visceral, unspeakable way. Somehow that seems lacking in the stripped-down modern Christian tradition often experienced today. There is a lack of mystery, a lack of beauty, a lack of something, as if I were watching TV with the sound off, or eating a steak with a stuffy nose. The language of visual art and beauty are missing, or at least somewhat askew.

I remember there was a life-sized crucifix that hung center stage, high above the altar. A statue of Jesus hung on that enormous cross. Eyes closed, His lean body limp and worn, a crown of thorns on His head, the pain and suffering and love pouring from His face, the statue was a longtime fixture in that church. And as such, it went largely ignored by the congregation. But it was there at the front of the church, upon marble steps, that I would kneel and stare up at this statue. And be in awe.

There in my little place, I would ponder God and the mystery of His grace. I would feel it, imagine it, sense it. As I saw the nails in His hands, I could almost hear the sound of the hammer. As I reflected on the crown of thorns, I could imagine the whips on His back. I pictured Jesus, placing Himself on the cross, opening His hands to accept the nails, fulfilling the promise. It was very surreal. And there was a real spiritual mystery to it too, that God the Son would do such a thing. How did He become man? Why would He choose to die like that? When will He return?

I remember I would pray, and my little prayers would just naturally stop, as my eyes continued to be drawn upward, to be in awe at the sight of Jesus on that cross.

Now I don't bring this up in order to entertain a theological debate about statues and icons. But I think there is a truth here, and it is this: We humans were created to grapple with the mysteries of the universe, and to be in awe and wonder at the sight of them. There are places in our heart for feelings like this. We need to feel them, imagine them, sense them. About God. About His creation. Because the sense of awe is inherent to the act of worship.

The uniquely inventive C. S. Lewis is one of the most influential Christian writers of the twentieth century. Penning such apologetic classics as *The Problem of Pain* and *Mere Christianity*, he is most known for the seven children's books that comprise The Chronicles of Narnia, a series that has been translated into more than thirty languages and has sold more than 85 million copies. Author, Oxford scholar, radio personality, Lewis was broadly read, broadly written, and broadly lived.

In the book *The Narnian: The Life and Imagination of C. S. Lewis*, writer and literature scholar Alan Jacobs contends that the key to Lewis was his willingness to "be delighted to the point of self-abandonment." In spite of his intellect and position, in spite of the tragedies and challenges he faced, he chose to live with the faith and eyes of a child. Jacobs writes:

> I want to suggest that Lewis's willingness to be enchanted held together the various strands of his life: his delight in laughter, his willingness to accept a world made by a good and loving God, and his willingness to submit to the charms of a wonderful story. What is "secretly present in what he said about anything" is an openness to delight, to the sense that there's more to the world than meets the jaundiced eye, to the possibility that anything could happen to someone who's ready to meet anything. For someone with eyes to see and the courage to explore, even an old wardrobe full of musty coats could become the doorway to another world.[2]

Lewis understood the ultimate triumph of childlike wonder in a world created and controlled and sustained by a benevolent, almighty Father. For it is true that our world is enchanted and supernatural and brimming with Godness. Like Lewis, we need to put away our jaded glasses, our sour dispositions, our worldly pessimisms, and put ourselves in places where we can genuinely say, "Ommagosh, it's bootiful."

We need to find the place in our hearts where we can be in awe. Because it fills our souls. It gives us hope. It reminds us of our place in the world. And it's good practice. For those of us who declare that heaven is our real home, awe and wonder and mystery will be a regular part of life.

Things I am in awe of now: The stars. Art and music. The ocean. God's grace.

MUSIC THEORY 101

In a previous life, I was a rocket scientist. Actually, I was a rocket engineer for ten years. I have a bachelor of science degree in aeronautical engineering from California Polytechnic State University, San Luis Obispo, and during that time, I spent two years working for the Air Force at Edwards Air Force Base, running computer models of rocket plumes. After I graduated, I moved to the Sacramento, California, area, and spent eight years working for an aerospace company as a rocket engineer for advanced concepts and as a program manager.

So whenever someone says, "It doesn't take a rocket scientist to play rock and roll," I smile.

Now the reason why I reveal this part of myself is because I have a theory. A pseudo-scientific theory. And it goes like this.

No one will argue that there is something about music that can profoundly and mysteriously move people—emotionally and spiritually. There is great beauty in the symphony, there is emotion in the aria, there is fire in the rock 'n' roll anthem, there is a God-breathed anointing in a hymn like "Amazing Grace."

But if you think about it, the physics of music is startling. *Sound* is the perception of minute gradations of pressure in the air, of energized air molecules traveling in waves. These waves enter your ears, vibrate the organs in your inner ear, and turn into electrical impulses that are interpreted by your brain as sound. *Pitch* is perceived by the frequency of the wave. *Timbre* is the complexity of the wave. (The mathematician Fourier actually discovered that any sound wave can be modeled by the addition of various sine waves alone . . . wild!) This is why we know the difference in sound quality between a trumpet and a clarinet, even if they play the same note. *Harmony* is perceived because we implicitly understand the intervals between frequencies. For example, the top note of an octave is exactly twice the frequency the bottom note. Concert pitch is often defined by setting the "A" note above "middle C" to 440 hertz, or vibrations of sound waves per second. The "A" above that is exactly 880 hertz, and the "A" below is exactly 220 hertz, and so on. And our human bodies are able to perceive the difference, even to less than a single hertz. *Rhythm* is the time intervals between sound waves. And music is the perception of pitch, timbre, melody, harmony, and rhythm all together.

We hear these changes in pitch, timbre, melody, harmony, and rhythm—and it makes us tap our toes, hum along, bop our heads up and down, even laugh and cry and get goose bumps. Such is the power and beauty of this phenomenon called music.

Consider the intentionality that God must have had in the creation of music. He created the atmosphere at sea level with a particular density to carry sound waves. (Contrary to the hundreds of science-fiction movies, there is no sound in outer space.) He created the means upon which objects can vibrate, like the double reed of an oboe or the stretched goatskin of a djembe or the vocal cords of a soprano or the catgut of a violin bow rubbing the strings. He created the human ear, an incredibly complex and intricate human subsystem for perceiving that sound. He created a capacity within the human brain to register these sound waves and turn them into electrical impulses and distinguish and organize sounds, an amazing feat unto itself.

> MY THEORY IS THIS: GOD LOVES MUSIC.

And then the most amazing thing of all: He created an inborn aesthetic within man that allows us to be moved by the beauty of form that comes from harmonic and rhythmic proportion. We hear music, and we feel sadness or joy, calmness or intensity, inspiration or transcendence.

I truly believe that those who look at the complexity of such things and do not see the intentionality behind it are simply fooling themselves. Thomas Dubay, in his book *The Evidential Power of Beauty*, states:

Computers cannot be constructed by random particles flying about for billions of years. The complete works of William Shakespeare, nicely printed and produced in a handsome volume, did not result from a gigantic explosion in a cosmic print shop eons ago. Winds and rains and dust blowing over and upon a large piece of marble did not bring the Pieta[3] into being. No normal person has the least doubt about these three statements. People know that chance can explain neither beauty nor intricate complexity.[4]

Now consider this. The book of Revelation describes music in heaven. People and heavenly beings singing praises to God. Music wondrous and beautiful and awe-filled beyond our wildest imaginings. God's intentionality of music extends to the supernatural places, toward heaven itself.

My theory is this: God loves music. He is passionate about it. He is the original audiophile. And more so, it is one of His love languages. He is moved by it. He is delighted by it. He derives great joy when we express ourselves to Him with music. He inspires us to sing, and we sing. He inspires us to compose and play, and we compose and we play. And He inspires us, in part because He simply loves to hear us play, loves to hear us compose, loves to hear us sing.

Do we as musicians truly understand this? Do we truly fathom this revelation? We musicians were created, in part, to play the gig to end all gigs. We have the privilege and honor of playing and singing for the God of the universe. And when we play and sing and worship, He taps His foot to the beat. He smiles at the clever turn of the phrase. He anticipates the key change, hangs on every note in the solo, leans forward in His seat when we hit the final chorus. He applauds when we finish each song. And we must never take that privilege lightly.

SEARCHING FOR TRANSCENDENCE

My freshman year in college, I went on tour with the Cal Poly Symphonic Band to Southern California. It was a big deal, because our tour culminated in a trip to Disneyland where we would play an afternoon concert in the Carnation Garden. In addition to being second-chair clarinet, I played in the Dixieland band (one of the skeletons in my closet), so I was pretty tired by the time we got to the Disneyland parking lot.

But we didn't enter the public entrance. Instead, we took a service entrance and found ourselves in a part of Disneyland I had never seen before. Hidden behind the well-manicured hedges and Park Employees Only signs, we found a back lot full of rusting Dumbo cars and broken carousel horses and other faded Disney-phernalia. It was drab, junky, unsettling, fallen, like we had crossed into Disney Hades. It was *not* a magical place.

Quickly we got off the bus, dressed, assembled, and tuned up. Then we were led by some costumed hostesses through a maze of halls and doorways. And as I pushed my way through a hidden gate in the wall, I suddenly found myself in a beautiful garden with happy faces, beautiful scenery, and children with balloons. This was the Disneyland we knew and loved. So we took our places under the gazebo and after checking concert pitch, launched into a couple of well-prepared songs.

All was going well . . . until Mickey showed up.

Mickey Mouse, saucer ears wiggling, walked smack dab into the middle of our concert and started mugging for the crowd. It was amusing at first, but quickly became annoying. And he wouldn't go away. Our flustered conductor, not knowing what to do, started mugging with him. In the midst of this indiscretion, he offered the conductor's baton to Mickey. *Oh no,* I thought to myself. *Oh, no, no, no, no.*

Mickey quickly snatched the baton. Mickey jumped onto the conductor's platform. Mickey raised his arms. And we—like dogs responding to Pavlov's bell—automatically raised our instruments to our lips.

It was like that scary scene from *Fantasia,* and we were already neck-deep in the water.

Then Mickey gave the downbeat. And the most magical thing happened. The entire band, over seventy of us, began to play the Mickey Mouse theme. In the same key. At the same time. In the same tempo. With woodwind flourishes and cymbal crashes and brass syncopation. A song we had never played, never rehearsed, never even had sheet music for.

"Hey there, hi there, ho there, we're as happy as can be. M-I-C-K-E-Y! M-O-U-S-E!"

We ended with a sting, then quickly pulled our instruments down onto our laps. And we looked at one another with shocked, puzzled looks on our faces, as if to ask, "Did that just happen?" Amidst the cheering, Mickey politely handed the baton back to our conductor, who was just as flabbergasted as we were. Then Mickey waved his big four-fingered gloves at the crowd, pulled on his suspenders, and disappeared with his entourage.

To this day, I have no explanation for what happened. I don't even remember the rest of the concert. But I will remember that moment for the rest of my life.

I believe the power of art lies in its transcendence. In the act of art, there is a mysterious, unquantifiable convergence between this world and the next. We feel it when we allow the silence of an oil painting to touch us. We feel it when we allow ourselves to be immersed in a symphonic performance. We feel it when we are pulled into a compelling movie. It's the same feeling when we grasp the beauty of a sunset or the power of the ocean or the awe of a shooting star.

For there is something deep within us that belongs more to the eternal than the temporal. Our soul longs for the supernatural, the spiritual, the things of heaven. And art is a language of the soul, allowing us to express that longing and pull back the curtain of the eternal window.

Jeremy Begbie asserts in his book *Voicing Creation's Praise*:

> I can see no compelling reason why the arts should not be approached from this perspective, or, to be more specific, why we should construe art as constantly moving us beyond this material world to some "higher" realm, or see the heart of an artist's work as giving outward expression to inner, non-material realities, as if the "real" work was

carried out in the sanctuary of the self, and the piece of art merely served to externalize and convey this inner experience.[5]

We are moved by art, because the beauty of art reflects a Divine aesthetic placed deep within all of us, sinners and saints alike. It is still another aspect of His revelation, a part of the fingerprint He has left upon us, His mortal sculptures. And when that aesthetic is tapped, we feel it. For some of us with heightened artistic awareness, it is deeper than for others. But it is there just the same.

The Holy Spirit is alive and well, moving around us, and for some, within us. He prompts, moves, waits, reveals.[6] And in that revelation, we transcend our earthly lives and visit the eternal.

I feel this often when I lead my church in worship. We gather together as church leaders and produce our agendas, our programs, our plans. We set up and prepare and rehearse the band, the technical details, the choir, the drama team. And then somewhere down the line, God shows up and surprises us in the most unusual ways. Sometimes it is in planning. Sometimes it is in worship. Sometimes it is in the private worship before worship. But He keeps showing up, again and again and again. And for some strange reason, when He does, I am always somehow surprised.

In the art of worship, as in the art of life, and as in the art of art, we expect and experience transcendence. For art is a magical thing. But we have such a surprising and awe-filled God, that when He shows up, we are still blown away.

REFRIGERATOR ART

I am an art collector. But not in the pretentious "hang it in the living room to impress" kind of way. I keep my art at the bottom of my top dresser drawer in the bedroom. I've been collecting this art off and on now for about fifteen years, ever since my firstborn son could pick up a crayon. And four children later, I think I've amassed a pretty good collection.

You know what I'm talking about. This is the art of discovery, the art of innocence, the art of perpetual hope. Pictures of frilly hearts and horsies, stick figures of Mommy and Daddy, superheroes, and things somewhat indescribable. Imaginings of a universe where it's okay to color outside the lines, where it's okay for dogs to be green and sometimes have more than two ears.

Each picture has taken its turn hanging in my office or on the refrigerator door, to be acknowledged and appreciated, to be the fine-motor skills exercise of little fingers, to be the soul expression of a little heart.

And there is something alive about these pictures. Alive because the artist becomes alive in the creation, like a storyteller whose voice rises as she reaches the climax of her story, or a rose whose time comes to bloom. My sons and daughters have taken their turns making their imaginations come alive, turning blank pieces of paper into colored landscapes alive in their minds.

HE TAKES WHAT WE CREATE AND HANGS IT ON HIS REFRIGERATOR DOOR.

Sure, my collection won't hang in the Louvre. But they are precious works of art to me nonetheless. Because they were created for me, with love and care and childlike craftsmanship. They reflect the hand of the artist and the vision of his mind's eye. My love for this art is a reflection for my love for the artists, who are my children.

I think God is like that. For God is our Father, our Abba, our Intimate God, and we are His children, his beloved. "How great is the love the Father has lavished on us, that we should be called children of God! And that is what we are!" (1 John 3:1).

For He sees our compositions, our choreography, our creations, those expressions that come from our souls, created from our hands, works from which He is the ultimate inspiration. And the Master Artist smiles at the creation of His creation. He genuinely takes pleasure in the work of our craft. He takes what we create and hangs it on His refrigerator door.

By definition, we all have artists in us, because we all see the world in our own special and distinct ways, and are able to express this view uniquely. Each of us sees the sunset differently. Each of us feels sadness differently. Each of us sees the color red differently. The smell of bacon and eggs in the morning is a distinctly different experience for each of us, because we each bring our own senses, preferences, physicalities, and memories to the breakfast table. This is true for every experience we encounter in life.

WE ARE ALL BORN ARTISTS, BUT IN THE ACT OF LIVING, THE ARTIST IN MANY OF US DIES.

The way you feel on a windy autumn-leaves afternoon, or when you sit at the beach and watch the ocean, or when you hear a baby laugh—all point to the artist that resides in you. The term is not reserved for the select few. For we all have been given the eyes and ears and hands and the souls of artists. And this is what makes this profound to me: that is how God made us.

But there is something terribly wrong with what we do with this Truth. You see, we grow up. And we learn that we are not artists, not really, for the term "artist" is something reserved for museums or people who produce albums. Somewhere in our journey, we learn that our art is somehow not good enough, and we put down the crayons and the paintbrushes, not wanting to embarrass ourselves. Or we learn that to be an "artist" is not to be a man, or to be responsible, or to be financially prudent, or some other label associated with the word, the concept. We put that label away. Madeleine L'Engle asserts that "only the most mature of us are able to be childlike."[7] We are all born artists, but in the act of living, the artist in many of us dies. And that is a shame.

It is like the little girl who asked her father what he did during the day, and he, being an art instructor, told her he taught people how to draw. "You mean, people forget?" was her honest reply.

I have met many people like this. People who are dying inside, dying to express something that comes from a place deep within, but have no way to express it. We die these little deaths, those of us who stopped taking piano lessons as a child, stopped doodling in the margins of our school papers, hung up their ballet shoes at an early age.

I have a friend who is a rocket engineer. But when no one is looking, he takes out his pastels and paints beautiful outdoor scenes and still art. I encouraged him once to display some of his pieces for an upcoming art gallery at our church. So he showed me a painting of a flower and then confided in me half-jokingly, "Don't tell the guys, okay?"

I get to know these people, those who are trying to find the artist inside of them, and I see their internal passion. They might not even be able to articulate this gnawing at their soul, but it is there just the same. And I have encouraged them—to find their voice, find their gift. And use it.

One person was a frustrated writer, but never really saw it as a gift until she was encouraged to stretch herself. Now she writes tremendously moving and insightful drama sketches and narratives. Another was a computer guy, a left-brained technical person who found out that he could be an artist in the theatrical arts. He learned to express himself through sound and lighting and video. Another person began taking a digital photography class, and the entire world opened up to her, for she saw the world in a whole different way than everyone else, but could never explain why or how. Now she can show to everyone the world that she sees, through the camera's eye.

If you ask any of these people, you discover that this is much more than finding a hobby. There is a connection to the soul in their art. And for each of these people I know, that connection is a vertical one.

I believe there is more to this than we even know. For God invites us—all of us, not just the privileged few—to meet Him in these places. He stirs us up and calls upon the artistic soul that is in every man and woman and child. He takes our crayon art, the creation of His creation, and holds it up to the light, and takes out His magnets, and hangs it on His refrigerator door.

• • •

Summary

In this first chapter, I hoped to give you a sense of how I have come to see our small but significant place in the universe with respect to God. For to understand our place as artists before God is to begin to see Him in a more full, more real, more true way. At the end of each chapter of this book, you will find a loose framework of the thoughts and ideas I've put forth. The following is a summary of our first chapter, God the Artist:

- ⸱ God is the Creator, the Master Artist. Birthed from His very nature, He created the universe and the world as we know it. And He derives pleasure from His creation, His Art (Genesis 1:1−31−2:1−2). Through the person of Jesus, all things were made and have their continuing coherence (John 1:1−3; Colossians 1:15−17; 1 Corinthians 8:6). As we are a part of His creation, we are both God's art, reflecting His image, and artists who reflect the image of God through our art.

- ⸱ We are made in God's image (Genesis 1:26). And as such, all of us are artists, as God is an Artist, endowed with both the ability and the passion to create, and the ability to derive pleasure from creating and creation. Human creativity is a part of the cultural mandate—to be fruitful and multiply, and to care for and steward the earth (Genesis 1:26−28; 2:19−20). Thus, artistry is intended for all of us, not just a select few.

- ⸱ God also created the unspoken aesthetic to which we aspire. We are endowed with an innate, mysterious understanding of this aesthetic (Romans 1:20), and thus we are moved by beauty and art, intellectually, emotionally, and spiritually. It is another aspect of us being made in God's image, and another aspect of God's revelation of Himself to the created universe.

֍ The mystery of this aesthetic is associated with transcendence, some avenue between this world and the eternal, and art is a language that allows us an avenue toward this transcendence. Our soul longs for the supernatural, the spiritual, the things of heaven, for we belong to the eternal. And art is a language that allows us to express and interact with that longing.

֍ God is our Father (1 John 3:1–3). And in the same way we put our children's crayon art on our fridge, God derives pleasure from us as His artist children. His pleasure stems from the act of our creativity as well as from the creation itself. In a sense, we glorify Him through the re-creation of art.

Discussion Questions

1. Think about what it is that you do that is artistic or creative. Do you consider yourself an artist? Do you hesitate to use that term to describe yourself? If so, why?

2. "We are artists because God made us in His image, and He is the Creator God." How does that statement change the way you see God? How does that change the way you see yourself? How does that change the way you see your art?

3. Think about an artistic expression that deeply moved you (e.g., play, film, concert, song). Why were you moved? Do you think God is moved in that way?

4. Consider an instance when you were overcome by a sense of profound mystery. What was it about that moment that struck you? How did it make you feel? Do you think we've lost a sense of mystery in our lives?

5. Have you ever hung art on your refrigerator door? Whose art was it? Why was it significant enough for you to hang it up? Was it simply because of its beauty, or was there some other reason?

6. When was the last time that you sat and watched the sun set, or the ocean tide come in, or the stars shining at night? What would it be like to see all of the universe as an act of God's creation, made not only for His glory but for His enjoyment and ours as well?

Chapter 2

ART
and FAITH

WHAT IS ART?

One of my favorite television shows as a child was a cheesy martial arts drama called *Kung Fu*.[1] Set in the Wild West, the drama starred a slow-talking, peace-loving Shaolin priest whose apparent lot in life was to quietly impart Eastern wisdom and morality, and then completely *womp* on the bad guys. As a short, nerdy kid who was sometimes targeted by bullies, this show had a natural appeal to me (especially the *womping* part).

The program often drifted into flashbacks of our hero, the young Kwai Chang Caine, being schooled in his Shaolin monastery. His Master, a blind monk with a bad Chinese accent, would teach Caine the mysteries of life through a variety of enigmatic statements, not unlike sayings from fortune cookies. Before Mr. Miyagi ever gave advice to the Karate Kid, before Yoda ever jumped on the back of Luke Skywalker, even before there was a Kung Fu Panda, there was *Kung Fu*.

In one of the most played-out scenes, the Master would challenge his young, bald disciple with the phrase, "Snatch the pebble from my hand." But it was only over the course of many years of cryptic words of wisdom—and many badly acted episodes—that Caine would succeed.

Of course, grabbing the pebble was only a metaphor for the larger life lesson that comes from true wisdom.

What is art? It is a query without a definitive response, with opinions so large as to fill a library of books. It is something not easily answered without going on an extended journey of discovery. There are no pat answers. It is a "snatch the pebble from my hand" matter.

Now, the quest for the truth of such big thoughts doesn't often come from *looking* for the right answers, but in first asking the right questions. Like a student in freshman composition, I cruised the Internet and found dictionary.reference.com, which supplied me with a handful of definitions:

"Human effort to imitate, supplement, alter, or counteract the work of nature."[2]

This is adequate as a somewhat-clinical definition, but it seems without soul and thus woefully lacking. For one, it doesn't take into account the *why*. Where does inspiration fit into this definition? What about imagination? What about incarnation?

"The conscious production or arrangement of sounds, colors, forms, movements, or other elements in a manner that affects the sense of beauty, specifically the production of the beautiful in a graphic or plastic medium."[3]

It is interesting to have the word *conscious* in this definition. I suppose I've never created art when I was unconscious—although I believe my subconscious plays a large part in my creation. I have awoken from dreams with almost fully formed songs in my head. And what about the word *beauty*? Thinkers have pondered the meaning of that word for thousands of years. There is much to be said about beauty, which is closely associated with art, though not synonymous with it. So we will attempt to grapple with the subject of beauty later in this chapter.

"The study of these activities."[4]

I'm not sure I can agree with this definition. Studying art may be art, but studying the activity of art probably is not. There are people who can talk about art, who are knowledgeable about art, and who can explain and critique art. But they are in danger of turning their experience to the academic and cerebral. They've forgotten that art is an expression of the heart, like the chef who can judge a great dish

WHO DECIDES WHAT IS EXCELLENT AND WHAT IS MEDIOCRE?

from a good one, but has somehow forgotten that the best meal is one shared with a friend.

"The product of these activities; human works of beauty considered as a group."[5]

Obviously, the product of creative effort can be deemed art. And you can categorize groups of art—like pottery, dance, music—as art. But that opens up a whole different set of questions. What activities can be deemed art? Is there an art to cooking? Landscaping? Boat-making? Accounting?

"High quality of conception or execution, as found in works of beauty; aesthetic value."[6]

Now we start to talk about quality, about aesthetics. What a can of worms! Is bad art still art? If the created work isn't "beautiful," is it still considered art? What if it is purposely not beautiful, but it evokes emotion; is it art or not? Who decides what is quality, what is excellent and what is mediocre? Where in man's psyche does that come from anyway? We will discuss this later in this chapter as well.

And where does our aesthetic come from? Is it learned, endowed by the communal consciousness that springs from culture over the course of generations? Or is it, as I suspect, placed within us at our creation? Our God has, as a part of His nature, the unspoken aesthetic to which we aspire. And then, because we are made in His image, He endows us with a mysterious understanding of this aesthetic.

"A nonscientific branch of learning; one of the liberal arts. A system of principles and methods employed in the performance of a set of activities: the art of building. A trade or craft that applies such a system of principles and methods: the art of the lexicographer. Skill that is attained by study, practice, or observation: the art of the baker; the blacksmith's art."[7]

There is definitely skill, including principles and methods, associated with the craft of making good art. I don't think good art just happens. I believe that there is typically a price to be paid for it. For myself, it was hundreds of hours behind a piano, practicing Czerny and scales and learning jazz substitution chords. For others, it was a thousand pieces of paper wadded and discarded in a wastebasket, or a thousand hours on the ballet barre.

My son Eric once complained that practicing his scales on his bass guitar was hard. I replied, in a most Dad-like voice, "Of course it's hard. If it were easy, everyone would do it."

My Internet surfing safari doesn't yield a sufficient definition. As one would expect, the dictionary gives only an academic definition of art. But what do artists say that art is? This is where art is lived, where art is alive. So once again, I hang ten on my virtual surfboard, and go to thinkexist.com for answers.

The results are surprising, confusing, enlightening, inspiring. Like so many words of wisdom from so many Masters. So snatch the pebble from my hand, as we read on.

"Art expresses man."[8]

Shinichi Suzuki
Violinist and inventor of the Suzuki Method

"Creativity is allowing yourself to make mistakes. Art is knowing which ones to keep."[9]

Scott Adams
American cartoonist

"Art is essentially the affirmation, the blessing, and the deification of existence."[10]

Friedrich Nietzsche
German classical philosopher

"All art is at once surface and symbol. Those who go beneath the surface do so at their peril."[11]

Oscar Wilde
Irish poet, novelist, and dramatist

"In art the hand can never execute anything higher than the heart can inspire."[12]

Ralph Waldo Emerson
American essayist

"We all know that Art is not truth. Art is a lie that makes us realize the truth, at least the truth that is given to us to understand."[13]

Pablo Picasso
Spanish painter

"Art does not reproduce the visible; rather, it makes visible."[14]

Paul Klee
Swiss artist

"Life doesn't imitate art, it imitates bad television."[15]

Woody Allen
American comedian, playwright, and actor

"Art enables us to find ourselves and lose ourselves at the same time."[16]

Thomas Merton
American monk

"Music is your own experience, your own thoughts, your wisdom. If you don't live it, it won't come out of your horn. They teach you there's a boundary line to music. But, man, there's no boundary line to art."[17]

Charlie Parker
American jazz musician

"What is Art ? It is the response of man's creative soul to the call of the Real."[18]

Rabindranath Tagore
Indian poet and playwright

FRAMING OUR ART

In my quest to define art, I am left with opinion. But there seems to me more truth in opinion than in the dictionary definition. So I will attempt to give you mine.

Art is an *expression*. It is a means by which we attempt to interpret and re-create the world God made. It is a language that expresses the human condition and seeks to make sense of it. It is, as Ken Gire states in his book of the same title, "windows of the soul."[19] In my own experience, playing the piano allows me to express the things of my heart that I cannot express verbally.

Art is a *discipline*. The Latin word for "art" is *tecnicus*, from which we derive the word *technique*. Art is something that must be developed and honed and rehearsed, in order to attain skill and competency. Artists must spend time playing to the metronome, or bending over the ballet barre, or developing the calluses of a sculptor. It is part of our calling. Although I believe I was endowed with a gift for music, the gift does not negate the hundreds of hours practicing on that old upright piano in our living room. Rather, God's gift to me obligated me to practice, so that I might steward that gift properly.

Art is *transcendent*. Art takes us someplace, spiritually as well as emotionally. It requires inspiration from God (for God is the ultimate source of inspiration for all art), and it is also a response to that inspiration. Art is, as Jeremy Begbie asserts, "capable of affording genuine knowledge of reality beyond the confines of human self-consciousness."[20] It is a means of tapping into the Unspoken Real. It is a transcendence that is more spiritual than we understand. Sometimes, playing the piano for me is as much meditation as it is music. However, it is up to us, through our free will, to respond to that inspiration— to either glorify the Source of inspiration, or glorify ourselves.

Art is *revelation*. Art points to something. It reveals. It can reveal both good and evil, beauty and ugliness, grace and mercy, injustice and sin. And if the artist is true to his or her art, it will reflect the artist's unique perspective on the world. Just as beauty in nature points to the reality of God, I believe that the beauty of art can point to God.

BEAUTY AND THE BEAT

When pondering a theology of art, there is a second, underlying issue that we've already touched on briefly. One cannot go far in the quest without at some point attempting to understand it. The issue is this: What is beauty? What is this quality that inspires the sonnet and soothes the savage beast and launches a thousand ships? This is a very big question, one that has stirred the hearts of philosophers much smarter than I, from Socrates to Buddha to Einstein. So I won't pretend to *know*. And I certainly won't be exhaustive about it. But I think it is extremely important to understand it.

First off, I think we must resist the temptation to adopt the lie of the cliché. Beauty is not in the eye of the beholder. Beauty is not subjective, in other words, dependent on the whims of the observer. Beauty is, in the more deeply philosophical sense, objective, a universal norm that crosses the boundaries of history and culture. Consider the wide variety of visual art styles, from the traditional Japanese art of *sumi-e*[21] or the art of the Renaissance or the mosaics of the Byzantine era or the work of some of today's digital, Photoshop artists. Or consider the vast diversity of architectural styles, from the Egyptian pyramids to the Taj Mahal to the Roman Coliseum to the works of Frank Lloyd Wright. Consider the expansive contrast of musical styles, from classical music to the myriad of Latin genres to Celtic folk music to that of the modern Broadway musical. Although the styles of each of these are vastly different, they each contain characteristics of beauty that are universal. For all of these expressions have the capacity to move us now artistically as they did in their own time and culture. There is an innate understanding within us all of the beauty of a sunrise, or a baby, or a landscape, or the lilies of the field. And this understanding is universal, more a property of the object of beauty than in the eye of the beholder.

SCIENCE IS BEGINNING TO UNDERSTAND IN DEEPER WAYS OUR NEED FOR FORM, AND BY IMPLICATION, BEAUTY.

The reason why beauty is objective is because beauty is a quality dependent on and relating to *form*. Beauty comes in intricacy, in elegance, in pattern, in arrangement. The form of a Shakespearean sonnet gives it beauty. The form of a Mozart concerto as well. The same is true for Tchaikovsky's *Swan Lake* ballet, the Beatles' *Sgt. Pepper* album, the wings of a butterfly, and Einstein's theory of relativity. Even in apparent chaos, there can be beauty when form underlies it: consider a spider's web, the growth of fungi, the works of Jackson Pollock, or even the arrangement of the stars in the universe. All have an apparent randomness, yet there is intricate substance of form, and thus beauty.

Think about that which you would consider beautiful, and you will see that form is embedded in it. We humans are drawn to form. We seek it, desire it, react to it, even require it to survive. And it is the premeditated form of the things of this universe that give it beauty and point people to God, the Beauty Maker.

Science is beginning to understand in deeper ways our need for form, and by implication, beauty. Recent studies show that people are highly sensitized to symmetry in judging human beauty. Others contend that there is a correlation between our universal aesthetic and our ability to process information; symmetry and form are more pleasing in part because they require less data processing from the observer. And it was Leonardo da Vinci and others who first tried to define beauty as a function of proportion of form.

Interestingly, scientists and mathematicians use beauty as an indicator of factual truth. Just look at the double helix, the elegant solution proposed to model the complexity of DNA. Paul Dirac, a Nobel Prize winner for his work in quantum physics, stated, "It is more important to have beauty in one's equations than to have them fit experiment." Buckminster Fuller, the out-of-the-box designer and futurist who invented the geodesic dome, once said, "When I'm working on a problem, I never think about beauty. I think only how to solve the problem. But when I have finished, if the solution is not beautiful, I know it is wrong."[22] And English mathematician and philosopher Bertrand Russell once remarked, "Mathematics possesses not only truth, but also supreme beauty." Scientists and mathematicians know implicitly that beauty is characterized by an elegance of form, and it is this form that points to truth.

Now, what we tend to see as subjective can be better described as "style." One can argue that it is really style that is in the eye of the beholder. One can paint a bowl of fruit in the simple elegance of *sumi-e* or reproduce it as a colorful Photoshop-enhanced still life or capture it in startling Ansel Adams black and white. And one can personally prefer one style over another. In fact, that is our nature, to not only prefer certain styles but to define one's individuality according to them. But beauty is still inherent to the art if it is expressed well, and we intrinsically know it and are moved by it. Style, like fashion, changes with time and culture.

Consider the hundreds of different styles of music. So many people discount certain styles of music (e.g., country or opera) without even understanding them. But I always insist that there are lots of musical styles, but only two musical types: good music and bad music. For there is good reggae, good new wave, good country, even good rap, just as there is bad classical, bad Broadway, and bad opera. So listen to the good stuff, regardless of the style.

So what is beauty? In an eloquent article entitled "The Art of Making Life Beautiful," author Catherine Michaud describes her view:

> In my search for a definition of beauty, I found the word kalos, which in classical Greek is one of the noblest of words; all through its long history, it has retained a certain splendor. It originally referred to a beauty of form, but the use of kalos ranges wide.... The early Christians used this Greek word, kalos, translated as beauty, but its usage expands our notion of beauty. It is used in the New Testament not fewer than one hundred times, usually to describe a characteristic quality of the Christian life. It describes that which commands love and admiration, that which is useful and honorable, that which is honest and winsome. It connotes the goodness... which not only satisfies the conscience, but which also delights the heart and gives pleasure to the eyes. Salt is said to be kalos. The Law of God is kalos. The word of God is kalos.[23]

It is important to understand the difference between beauty and art. If art is an expression of the soul, then art can be beautiful, but it need not be. Art can express ugliness, perversity, and chaos, and be good art, if it is created with craftsmanship and skill and integrity. And beauty doesn't have to be art either. Indeed, beauty extends beyond art. There is beauty in all of nature. There is beauty in the character of Mother Teresa. There is beauty in the Great Commandment. There is beauty in the Trinity. There is even beauty in the honest portrayal of pain, hurt, fear, and other aspects of the human condition. Beauty, then, is related to art, in that it is a quality that can be found within the expression of art. But they are different things.

Now, why is understanding beauty important in understanding a theology of art?

There is such a thing called "sympathetic resonance." When one plays a string on a guitar or a piano, there are fundamental and harmonic vibrations taking place, usually measured in beats per minute. The harmonic vibrations are sympathetic; in other words, if there is a string whose inherent frequency is mathematically and physically harmonic to the string that is vibrating, then that string will want to vibrate also. Guitarists use this little fascinating physics phenomenon when they play harmonics.

I believe that we, as God's creation, are endowed with a spiritual sympathetic resonance too. And that resonance is in part through beauty. Psalm 19 states, "The heavens tell of the glory of God. The skies display his marvelous craftsmanship. Day after day they continue to speak; night after night they make him known. They speak without a sound or a word; their voice is silent in the skies; yet their message has gone out to all the earth, and their words to all the world" (vv. 1–4 NLT).

And the book of Romans declares: "From the time the world was created, people have seen the earth and sky and all that God made.

They can clearly see his invisible qualities—his eternal power and divine nature. So they have no excuse whatsoever for not knowing God" (Romans 1:20 NLT).

Try wrapping your brain around that one. Both the psalmist and the apostle Paul state that there are certain attributes of God embedded in the created order that point to Him. And then we, a part of creation, have the very beauty of creation placed into us, a resonant frequency to our souls. For our souls resonate with a heavenly aesthetic when we come before beauty. This is why we are drawn to the sight of a snowcapped mountain or the sound of a singing mockingbird. Gabriela Mistral, Chilean poet and Nobel Prize winner, stated eloquently, "Love beauty; it is the shadow of God on the universe."

I would go so far as to say that beauty is defined by God and by His original intentions of creation. And the subjective relativity that many see in Beauty and in Truth is a post-fall view held by those whose hearts are not necessarily aligned with God's heart. In a sense, their hearts are out of tune with the Divine resonance. For example, God intended the human form to be beautiful, and much of classical art assents to this. But pornography takes that beauty and creates dehumanizing and destructive perversity. God created music to ultimately glorify Himself; some musicians take music, and the power and beauty inherent in it, and use it to ultimately glorify themselves.

The longing for the infinite and our longing for beauty is universal, and I believe, related. This is why it is important to understand the objectivity of beauty apart from the subjectivity of our personal experiences of it. In a sense, it is not beauty that is subjective, but our response to it, which is a result of free will—those whose hearts are out of frequency with the fundamental frequency, whose hearts don't beat as God's heart beats. Because God is the author of beauty. And He is the inventor of the unspoken aesthetic within us that resonates with beauty.

We feel this deep within us in ways we do not even understand. Thomas Dubay contends:

> You and I, each and every one of us without exception, can be defined as an aching need for the infinite. Some people realize this; some do not. But even the latter illustrate this inner ache when, not having God deeply, they incessantly spill themselves out into excitements and experiences, licit or illicit. They are trying to fill their inner emptiness, but they never succeed, which is why the search is incessant. . . . If these people allow themselves a moment of reflective silence (which they seldom do), they notice a small voice whispering, Is this all there is? They begin to sense a thirst to love with abandon, without limit, without end, without lingering aftertastes of bitterness. In other words, their inner spirit is clamoring, even if confusedly, for unending beauty. How they and we respond to this inner outreach rooted in our deep spiritual soul is the most basic set of decisions we can make: they have eternal consequences.[24]

Of course, the thirst for beauty that he speaks of is ultimately a spiritual one. It is what made the psalmist pen: "One thing I have asked from the Lord, that I shall seek: That I may dwell in the house of the Lord all the days of my life, to behold the beauty of the Lord and to meditate in His temple" (Psalm 27:4 NASB). For ultimately, God is the author of beauty. And anyone who is moved by beauty is closer to God than they realize.

ART AND THE CHRIST-FOLLOWER

The Old Testament Israelites had a long-standing relationship with art. Although God forbade the making of any carved images or likenesses that would be worshiped (Exodus 20:4–5), He did not forbid artistic expression. Actually, the contrary. God commanded that He be worshipped in a tabernacle brimming with artistic expressions, including carvings, tapestries, sculptures, metalwork, furniture, and architecture. There were images of lions, palm trees, bulls, cherubim, birds, and other things in the tabernacle (Exodus 25; 1 Kings 7). And the Israelites' worship was punctuated with songs sung and played by many skilled musicians (more on this in chapter 3).

Biblical aesthetics are based on the theology of creation, in which we are free to create just as God created the universe—from nothing. As mentioned in chapter 1, human creativity is part of the cultural mandate: to be fruitful and multiply, and to care for and steward the earth (Genesis 1:26–28; 2:19–20). This command to "subdue" the earth includes a responsibility to cultivate, conserve, develop, and even to form, create, and imagine. The Christian tradition then accommodates most forms of art, including representational art as well as abstract art, fiction, fantasy, and allegorical art. This is in contrast to the Greek and Roman worldview, which was grounded in "mimesis," or imitation, in which the physical universe was regarded as an imperfect imitation of a previously existent ideal.

This Christian aesthetic developed over the course of two thousand years and gave rise to much religious classical art and music. Of course, the Reformation sparked a backlash against Roman Catholic practices of religious images, and there have been many Protestant limitations on art over the years. For example, Protestant Reformer and theologian John Calvin was purported to believe that artists should limit their art to only those things that could be seen. And there are other artificial impositions placed on art even today. But in my opinion, we as artists have the freedom to draw, paint, film, dance, relate, and compose, limited only by the imaginations and talents God has given us.

All freedoms come with inherent responsibilities and implications, and we as artists who are Christ-followers have ours as well. I've tried to define art, and taken a detour toward beauty. So what is our relationship to art? How are we, as artists saved by grace through Christ Jesus, to paint and dance and write and film and sing? Francis Schaeffer, in his seminal work *Art and the Bible*, contrasts different views of art. In one view:

> Art is only an embodiment of a message, a vehicle for the propagation of a particular message about the world or the artist or man or whatever. Christians as well as non-Christians have held this view, the difference between the two versions being the nature of the message that the art embodies. But, as I have said, this view reduces art to an intellectual statement and the work of art as a work of art disappears.[25]

In this view, art is simply a medium upon which truth is revealed, a vehicle for a message. But Schaeffer goes on to describe a larger view of art.

> [This] basic notion of the nature of art—the one that I think is right, the one that really produces great art and the possibility of great art— is that the artist makes a body of work and this body of work shows his worldview. . . . I emphasize the body of an artist's work because it is impossible for any single painting, for example, to reflect the totality of an artist's view of reality. But when we see a collection of an artist's paintings or a series of a poet's poems or a number of a novelist's novels, both the outline and some of the details of the artist's conception of life shine through.[26]

What Schaeffer says resonates with me, and it is this latter notion that has framed my own journey as an artist. Art should reflect the artist in some way—what he believes, what he has experienced, what he has placed his faith in, how he uniquely sees the world. And for the Christ-follower who is an artist, his worldview should reflect the creativity of the Abba Father, the Kingship of Jesus Christ, and the inspiration of the Holy Spirit.

I personally have received much freedom from this understanding of art and faith. Because we are not constrained to creating music that has to have a "message." Because what Schaeffer implies is that we as artists can glorify God simply in the creation of our art. We are like the flowers of the field, each of which glorifies our God simply by being what He created it to be. God created us to be artists, and thus we give God glory by simply exercising the act of creativity. St. Irenaeus stated, "The glory of God is a man fully alive." And we artists do feel more fully alive in the act of creation, don't we? It is like the scene in *Chariots of Fire*, when Eric Liddell declares that "when I run, I feel His pleasure." Our maturity in Christ—as well as our maturity as artists— might then be measured in part by our ability to feel God's pleasure in the act of creation.

I am not at all discounting those who use their art as a means to an end, e.g., to evangelize. I knew a very gifted "musicianary" in Spain who used his gifts in large part to further outreach efforts in his corner of the world. He wrote inventive original music and covered lots of other material, played to some extremely diverse audiences in many countries, and then told them about Jesus. And although I would categorize a lot of what he did as falling into the second category of Schaeffer's statement above, there is nothing inauthentic about him. He simply loves God and music, and shares both wherever he goes.

What I am referring to is the authentic expression of who one is. Above all, one's art should spring from this place. If it is true, and if it is good, there will be those who will be moved by it.

King David was deep in the desert of Judah when he composed this sonnet:

> O God, you are my God, earnestly I seek you; my soul thirsts for you, my body longs for you, in a dry and weary land where there is no water. I have seen you in the sanctuary and beheld your power and your glory. Because your love is better than life, my lips will glorify you. I will praise you as long as I live, and in your name I will lift up my hands. (Psalm 63:1–4)

David wasn't hoping to write a hit song. He was simply sharing the deep spiritual desires of his heart at a time when he really needed to hear from God. And in that raw honesty, he penned something that has touched generations of the faithful. That and the rest of the Davidic Psalms are, in essence, what Schaeffer is talking about.

There are some who set out to create "Christian art." Consider the proliferation of CCM, contemporary Christian music, as if it were an actual musical style, like country music or blues. Or consider the Christian bookstore industry, Christian radio, Christian Yellow Pages, or other Christian subcultural expressions. Now I don't necessarily have anything against any of these things—I know good people in the contemporary Christian music industry, I frequent Christian bookstores, I read Christian books, and I have been known to wear the occasional T-shirt with a Christian symbol on it. Still, there is something unintended but insidious in the subculture of "Christian art." Because inbred in it is a form of sectarianism, which seeks to separate itself from the world. For the world is a nasty place, with critics and cretins and consumers, and it is safer to write music for the chosen, for the already convinced, lest we pollute ourselves. This sectarianism marginalizes art by labeling it and valuing it according to its apparent spirituality rather than its artistry. (This is in essence a form of the first notion stated by Francis Schaeffer previously.) Unfortunately, in the worst case, you end up with religious platitudes wrapped in watered-down art.

I meet musicians like this all the time. They are constantly calling me, asking if we would like them to perform during a church service. They send me slick promo kits with glowing testimonials from pastors about their walk with God, their ministry to the church. And unfortunately, much of their music is pretty average. They simply haven't allowed themselves to be challenged by the greater worldview of art.

The other effect of sectarianism is that we as artists never end up making a difference in the world. Rather than joining the potpourri of worldviews (for the Christian faith can make a legitimate, rational, artistic, and compelling stand with any other worldview), Christian artists are reduced to ghettoizing our art. This is why Christian recording artists have their music tucked away in the "inspirational" section of the record store instead of within the pop, rock, and other genres. By doing so, it marginalizes the artist as well. This has been a continuing frustration for me, as I don't feel I need to write spiritually acceptable music that conforms to various unstated norms or formulas. I personally don't believe that is my calling, and I feel it would be disingenuous to do so.

> WE TRY AS ARTISTS TO BE TRUE TO WHO WE ARE CALLED TO BE. AND IN THE PROCESS, WE TOUCH SOME AND NOT OTHERS.

In *Voicing Creation's Praise*, author Jeremy Begbie reflects:

> A Christian painter recently wrote that "once the pressure is there to make a painting 'message-oriented' there is a strong tendency to undervalue or ignore the reality of a painting as a painting." . . . And in

worship, especially in the Protestant West, the representative arts are frequently seen as a kind of ornament, a decorative substitute for what can be plainly stated, a colourful wrapping to attract people's attention, dispensable when the "real" truth appears elsewhere in the service (usually in a sermon). Such a view implies that works of art are essentially dressed-up statements, no more than thinly disguised or second-rate assertions.[27]

What is a Christian artist to do? I offer a simple answer: don't set out to create Christian art. Simply create art that is a true expression of the self. Don't fit someone's formula; create your own. Don't aspire to fame; aspire to authentic self-expression and artistry. Don't seek to "evangelize"; simply and authentically share your story. And if we are living authentically in the rule and reign and relationship of our Abba God, our faith will inherently manifest itself somehow in our art.

And really, isn't that art's more noble intention? We live, we love, we express ourselves. We try to be true to who we are, who we are called to be. And in the process, we touch some and not others.

One of the musical highlights of my life was playing in a jazz fusion group called Vespers. We were together as a group for seven years, released three CDs, played hundreds of gigs in the northern California area, and received modest airplay. We were offered one record deal (which we respectfully turned down). During our time together, I continually struggled with the label "Christian jazz" that people placed on us (and we inadvertently placed on ourselves). What did that mean anyway? Yes, we were a band of Christ-followers (at least four out of five of us were). And we sought to glorify God with our original music. But we played about half of our gigs for Christian organizations and the other half for nightclubs and festivals. Vespers was a first-call band for the top smooth jazz radio station in our area.

And we were a first-call band for the top Christian radio station as well. The thing of it was, we played the exact same music in both venues.

If Schaeffer is right—that the possibility of great art happens when the art reflects the artist's conception of life and faith—then this is the way art should happen. I know this to be true of me. And that is how I am true to myself and to God.

VAN GOGH, KING DAVID, AND ME

Some years ago, I was working a few projects with a recording engineer at a large studio in the area. He had been in Nashville, working his way up the music business food chain, but decided to move back to Sacramento after a number of years. So I asked him why. He told me that he had seen so many things in the business that soured him to Nashville, and he just couldn't take it anymore. Shady dealings, image management, lies, lawsuits, adultery, fornication, drugs. The thing of it was, he had experienced all of this from Christian artists.

DOES THE LIFE OF THE ARTIST NEGATE THE ART?

In another instance, I had booked a local Christian band to play during one of my church's midweek services. They had some good music and a touching testimony, and my congregation was really moved by their performance. I found out about six months later that the male and female vocalists in this group were having an affair. There are many other more public instances in the circle of Christian musicians that need not be named.

It used to surprise me when some Christian public figure didn't live up to his image, but it doesn't anymore. I think it's because I've come to the realization that we are all sinners, susceptible to the lies of Satan, the world, and ourselves, and having musical or other artistic talent doesn't safeguard us from our human carnality.

I'll be talking in more detail about the artist and sin in chapter 3.

What I wondered about for a long time, though, was the legitimacy of the art. Does the life of the artist negate the art? Where is the integrity of the art, if there is no integrity in the author of that art?

Probably the best example of an artist in the Bible is David. Author of many of the psalms, king of the nation Israel, slayer of Goliath, the poet-warrior, the one the Bible describes as being a "man after God's heart." And yet, he was an adulterer, a polygamist (although many would argue that polygamy was a politically and socially acceptable practice at that time), and the murderer of the husband of someone with whom he was having an affair. Yet his psalms have spoken deeply to me and to many others. As I have matured in my faith, I have been continually drawn to the person of David, relating to him on level upon level. His passion. His artistry. His sin.

Over time, I came to the conclusion that there has never been any art created by mortal man that hasn't been colored by sin in some way. I know that in my own life, I've never had a truly pure motivation. Everything I have ever done has been skewed in some way by my own neediness, my own selfishness, my own agenda, my own dysfunction. So why should anyone else, outside of Jesus Himself, be any different?

So there must be some aspect of art that has the potential for expression, interpretation, and ministry separate from the artist who created it. For art is a painting apart from the painter, a story apart from the storyteller, a melody apart from the composer. It is as if art has a life of its own, used by God at His discretion, for His purposes, in His timing. In a sense, art becomes self-existent, legitimate, alive. And we as artists have an obligation to birth the art and set it free.

> THERE HAS NEVER BEEN ANY ART CREATED BY MORTAL MAN THAT HASN'T BEEN COLORED BY SIN IN SOME WAY.

Vincent Van Gogh, that tortured painter known for chopping off part of his ear, was nonetheless an immensely talented and inspired artist. His paradigmatic work stands today as a definition of post-Impressionism. And my church has used his paintings as devotional art, pointing people toward the greater Truth that is in Christ Jesus. Arguably his most famous work is also my favorite, *Starry Night*. More than a picture, it is an alternative perspective, a unique interpretation of the universe. And it was painted by Van Gogh as he sat in the Saint-Paul-de-Mausole asylum at Saint-Remy-de-Provence.

Art can be and is used by God apart from the artist. In other words, the work of an artist can have meaning and ministry outside of the scope of the artist who created it. Because the nature of God is that He can not only redeem the artist, but in a sense, be redemptive in the work of the artist as well. He can use the work of a psychologically flawed, self-destructive painter in spite of himself. He can use the work of a sinful, prideful king in spite of himself. And He can use my music in spite of myself. Because the reason why does not lie in the author, but in the Inspirer of the author. God is the ultimate source of inspiration, the singularity upon which all inspiration is derived. He was the same God who inspired Van Gogh, inspired King David, inspires me.

I can imagine Van Gogh in his physical and emotional prison, struggling with the demons of his life, grasping at some greater Truth he cannot speak. From his window, he contemplates the twinkled night sky and sees God's revelation of creation. In this moment of clarity, he takes his brush in his hand. And out of the nothingness of that blank canvas, he carves out swirls of sky and points of light and shadows of a city in twilight.

In the depths of his own personal darkness, he births a masterpiece. And he sets it free.

PRODIGAL ART

I went through an interesting devotional exercise with my church's drama team once. I challenged everyone to share a story. It could be a film they had seen, a book they had read, even a bedtime story. The only prerequisite was that it had to mean something to them, had to have touched them somehow.

One by one, we went around the room, sharing our stories. A film (*A River Runs Through It*), a novel about the Second World War, an old classic western (*The Magnificent Seven*), and several other stories I can't remember. Some funny, some poignant. And as we completed the circle, I revealed my motive: each one of the stories shared that evening was a story of redemption. A story of someone who gained grace not deserved. A story where forgiveness was given and acceptance was received and reconciliation was shared.

Our society is full of redemption stories. We are drawn to them, be it *Rudolph the Red-Nosed Reindeer*, or Hans Christian Andersen's *Ugly Duckling*, or *Shrek*. Disney knows this and has even turned it into a formula. *Dumbo* is a classic tale of a young elephant ostracized by society because he doesn't fit in. But through a remarkable series of events, he redeems himself and becomes the most beloved elephant in the circus. Or how about *Pinocchio*, a classic tale of a puppet ostracized by society because *he* doesn't fit in? But through a remarkable series of events, he redeems himself and becomes the beloved son of his toymaker father. Or maybe we can look at *The Hunchback of Notre Dame*, the classic tale of a deformed orphan ostracized by society because he doesn't fit in. But through a remarkable series of events, he redeems himself and becomes the beloved bell ringer of the city. Or how about *Beauty and the Beast*?

The Bible too is full of redemption stories: Jacob, Joseph, Moses,

Ruth. And in the larger context, the story of God and the entire nation of Israel is a redemption story, for Israel is the prodigal people. Each of these real people had their stories, had their walks in the desert or their times of forsakenness, had their times of reflection and returning, had their times of acceptance and redemption. And there is a reason for this, I believe: God is in the business of redeeming people.

Probably the most famous of Jesus' parables is the archetype of the redemption story. It is most popularly known as "The Prodigal Son."

There was a man who had two sons. The younger one said to his father, "Father, give me my share of the estate." So he divided his property between them.

Not long after that, the younger son got together all he had, set off for a distant country and there squandered his wealth in wild living. After he had spent everything, there was a severe famine in that whole country, and he began to be in need. So he went and hired himself out to a citizen of that country, who sent him to his fields to feed pigs. He longed to fill his stomach with the pods that the pigs were eating, but no one gave him anything.

When he came to his senses, he said, "How many of my father's hired men have food to spare, and here I am starving to death! I will set out and go back to my father and say to him: Father, I have sinned against heaven and against you. I am no longer worthy to be called your son; make me like one of your hired men." So he got up and went to his father.

But while he was still a long way off, his father saw him and was filled with compassion for him; he ran to his son, threw his arms around him and kissed him.

The son said to him, "Father, I have sinned against heaven and against you. I am no longer worthy to be called your son."

But the father said to his servants, "Quick! Bring the best robe and put it on him. Put a ring on his finger and sandals on his feet. Bring the fattened calf and kill it. Let's have a feast and celebrate. For this son of mine was dead and is alive again; he was lost and is found." So they began to celebrate. (Luke 15:11–24)

The story is almost too good to be true. It is extravagant, lavish, grace filled. It reaches deep into our most inherent need—to feel unconditional love and inner healing and intimacy. It captures in us a hope that all is not lost, all is not faint stumbling in the darkness. In my own life, I have related to the prodigal, and to his overly righteous brother, and to his joyous father. The story is true. Because we all share in the story.

Henri Nouwen, in his book *The Return of the Prodigal Son*, recounts his spiritual encounter with the Truth while viewing Rembrandt's painting of the same name. So deep was his experience that he embarked on a pilgrimage of sorts to St. Petersburg to see the painting firsthand. In his journey, he came face-to-face with the startling Truth of the parable. He writes:

When I saw the Rembrandt poster for the first time in the fall of 1983, all my attention was drawn to the hands of the old father pressing his returning boy to his chest. I saw forgiveness, reconciliation, healing; I saw safety, rest, being at home. I was so deeply touched by this image of the life-giving embrace of father and son because everything in me yearned to be received in the way the prodigal son was received. That encounter turned out to be the beginning of my own return.[28]

There is power in the redemption story. And this is where art comes in. Because art is, in a sense, a story of redemption. We redeem the white canvas with lines and colors. We redeem the blank page with words and ideas. We redeem the empty stage with dance and movement. We redeem the silver screen with moving imagery. And in a larger sense, we redeem these empty places with our ideas, with our thoughts, with expressions of ourselves. And in that context, we tell the story of ourselves.

And here is the essence of our story: each of us is a prodigal son. Each of us is in the process of cooperating with or rebelling against God's redemptive hand in our lives. We are His redemption stories. And when we express our art, our lives shine through it. Our art reflects the story God writes of us. Madeleine L'Engle knew this and stated, "To paint a picture or write a story or to compose a song is an incarnational activity."[29] For it is a fleshing out of our faith.

The story of the universe—of all that we know, and don't know, and don't know we don't know—is in essence the story of God. God is at the center of all creation, perfect in His tri-unity, self-existent and almighty and eternally young, and by His very nature, He causes all things to be and sustains them by the mere act of His will. And our stories are small vignettes in this vast and eternal meta-narrative. We, as artists who follow Christ, need to tell our story, render our personal expressions of redemption to the world. And tell them with artistry and beauty and grace. And in doing so, we hint at the grander story of God.

• • •

Summary

This second chapter was a little more cerebral, though not at all comprehensive. (If you are interested in deeper material on these subjects, I suggest the books listed in the bibliography.) It was a necessary attempt to seek out the beginnings of truth from all the opinion out there, and provide some foundational ideas about art, beauty, style, and redemption. The following is a summary of some of the thoughts from our last chapter, Art and Faith:

- Art is an expression. It is a means by which we attempt to interpret or re-create the world God made.
- Art is also a discipline. It is something that must be developed and trained for in order to attain skill and competency.
- Art is transcendent. Art takes us someplace, spiritually as well as emotionally, a window between this world and the next. And art requires inspiration. Ultimately, God is the ultimate source of inspiration for all art. However, it is up to us, through our free will, to respond to that inspiration—to either glorify the Source of inspiration or glorify ourselves.
- Art is revelation. Art points to something. It is the artist's unique perspective on the world, which can reveal both good and evil, beauty and ugliness, grace and mercy, as well as injustice and sin.
- Beauty and art are related, but are different things. Beauty is an objective quality related to form, and not a subjective quality dependent on the beholder. True beauty is defined by God and by His original intentions of creation.
- Because God created us in His image, with an inborn aesthetic that is like His, we are drawn to and moved by beauty. Beauty,

and the whole universe, is a display of God's craftsmanship, and ultimately beauty points to God in a transcendent way (Psalm 19:1–4; Romans 1:20; Psalm 27:4; etc.).

§ Art can be and is used by God apart from the artist. In other words, the product of an artist can have meaning and ministry outside of the scope of the artist who created it. God can and does redeem not only the artist, but in a sense, the work of the artist as well. Artists have an obligation to create with authenticity and skill, to be servants of the work, to birth the work that is inspired by God.

§ "To paint a picture or write a story or to compose a song is an incarnational activity." Art should ultimately be an expression of our redemption stories, a fleshing out of our faith. For our stories hint at the larger meta-narrative, the story of God's redemption of the universe.

Discussion Questions

1. What is your definition of art? Do you think it is congruent with the idea that God is the Creator, the Artist God?

2. Think about something you believe is beautiful. Do you believe that beauty is objective (not dependent on what we think or feel) or subjective (in the eye of the beholder)?

3. Is beauty important to God? If so, why? Why is beauty important to us?

4. Think of an example of art that is used primarily as a vehicle for a message. Now think of an example of art that is primarily an expression of the human self or human condition. Contrast the two.

5. Think about a story (book, movie, play, etc.) that moved you. Was it a story of redemption?

6. If you are in a discussion group, take the time to briefly share the story that God has written of your life.

Chapter 3

The ARTIST *in* COMMUNITY

THE ART OF COMMUNITY

I once played at a local event with my band. It would prove to be a fun venue: a set of instrumental jazz during dinner, then a short concert of our original music before the keynote speaker was announced. It was for the worship arts ministry for a large church, so they were hip and responsive to the music we were sharing that evening. As the emcee for the evening prepared his remarks, he came to the sudden realization that he didn't know the name of our group. Slipping behind me as we played, he leaned into me as I dug into my piano. "What's the name of your band?" he shouted into my ear.

"Uh, the Manuel Luz Trio," I offered mid-solo.

"What?" he asked, probably expecting something more creative, like Big Toe and the Turnips or the Compunctions of Calypso.

With a single glance at Steve and Matt on drums and bass, respectively, I communicated the next solo over chorus, before turning back to the emcee. "We're just a trio," I replied. "The Manuel Luz Trio."

"Trio," he repeated, wanting to make sure it was right.

I caught a glimpse of Matt, and he nodded back to me, aware that I was asking him to take a bass solo, then turned back to the emcee, who had already begun to walk away. "Well, it's not rocket science," I said to myself, smiling.

There's nothing like jammin' in a jazz trio. Especially when the players are good and the band plays tight. There is an immediacy of every moment of every song. Every groove percolates. Every solo is an adventure. Every song is a work of art.

But it's not easy. First, you need players who really know how to listen. Jazz is, by definition, an art of improvisation. There is a risk, a freshness, a *now*, to every moment, like walking on a high wire. At any given moment, with any given note, you can fall right off. But when you are with real players who listen—really listen—then you can take chances with your solo, play outside, take risks. You are free to express, to invent, to create. And they will back you up, musically encouraging you and challenging you in the safety of "the band." The best drummer I ever had the honor of playing with had such great musicality, that every solo I took always sounded better, not because of me, but because of him.

It was as if each person in the band was not just playing the music— they had lived it.

There is also great dynamic range when you have players who listen. Songs crescendo and decrescendo, ebbing and flowing from verse to verse, solo to solo, as everyone in the band flies in formation, implicitly feeling the subtleties of intensity.

You also need players who are selfless. When you are with selfless players, everyone can take turns soloing. There is a mutual respect and submission to one another, as each person takes their solo. There is an appreciation for each person as their solo—their personal interpretation of the song—is quietly acknowledged and celebrated with a nod or a smile. There is forgiveness when you make mistakes, and in the immediacy of that moment, there is recovery, reinstatement, grace, and then the music goes on. And in the applause that follows a well played tune, there is the knowledge that the sum of the parts is greater than the whole.

And you need players who are passionate. Jazz without passion is elevator music. Like the guy in the tuxedo at the Ramada Inn playing sequenced Jobim. I mentioned earlier that I used to play in a Dixieland band in college and (believe it or not) I actually enjoyed it. But to tell you the truth, I didn't like listening to it very much. Dixie music just seemed like so many middle-aged white people playing at Main Street, U.S.A. Until I went to Bourbon Street, New Orleans.

In my previous life as an engineer, I was assigned to a feasibility study on the Space Shuttle, and I found myself on a business trip to Martin Marietta in Michoud. While I was there, I had the opportunity to sightsee at the famous Bourbon Street in New Orleans. After dinner, we went to Preservation Hall, an old, dilapidated building with holes in the planked floor. In this dimly lit venue, a half-dozen older black gentlemen sat on stage, playing the most soulful music I had ever heard. It was emotive, mournful, moving. It was as if each person in the band was not just playing the music—they had lived it. That's when I understood, for the first time, what Dixieland music was really about.

Here is the thing: I haven't been talking about jazz. To state the obvious, the jazz trio is a metaphor for biblical community. In true biblical community, there are all of these components: selflessness, dialogue, grace, mutual submission, synergy, improvisation, and shared passion. They are necessary—even commanded—in order to play the music that is the healthy, functional church. The church, the bride of Christ, is intended to birth the music that cares for the lost, loves the world, makes disciples, and worships the Living God. It is an improvised symphony, alive and breathing, bathed in the mystery and wonder of our shared journey with Him.

The biblical church isn't a building or an institution. Sure, there are church buildings and there exists the institution of the church, both of which are apparent necessities. But the church is, first and foremost, a community of Christ-following sinners who love God, love people, and live under His reign, His Kingdom.

The church, for all of its faults and foibles, is the bride of Christ. And when it plays its music, it is hope of the world. It was designed that way. And when it works right, there is nothing more beautiful and compelling.

A FISH IN WATER, A BEAR IN THE WOODS, ME AT MY PIANO.

There's nothing like jammin' in a jazz trio. Especially when the players are good and the band plays tight. There is an immediacy of every moment of every song. Every groove percolates. Every solo is an adventure. Every song is a work of art.

ART AND THE AUDIENCE

I love to play for an audience. There is something about the feedback, the immediacy, the intimacy. Whether I play for two or two thousand, there is this unspoken conversation between the performer and the audience that I love to share in. It's a dialogue that gives the artist permission to share his or her thoughts and feelings and expression, at the approval or disapproval of the public. And this dialogue is as much a part of the performance as what I sing or what piano keys I press.

I have felt at home on the stage since I was four years old. I would play piano recitals, community functions, Christmas and Easter programs, school shows, and for unsuspecting victims trapped in our living room. "Manny! Come out here and play something for your

Auntie!" As a little kid, I played Mozart and Chopin and Beethoven for people who didn't understand and sometimes didn't even care.

But that was okay by me; I was in my element. A fish in water, a bear in the woods, me at my piano. I learned early that my piano was capable of shielding me in my shyness while allowing me to express my emotion to an audience. Behind a piano, I felt free. I've been in bands practically my whole adult life. My wife knows this about me, and has quietly supported the many bands and recording projects I've been in over the years. So she is a band widow. And if you're married to a busy musician, you know what I mean.

In the previous section, I use the metaphor of the jazz trio to describe the intention of the universal church, how the synergy of shared passion, dialogue, and grace forms us as the body of Christ. Now I would like to speak specifically about the relationship between artists and their audience. There is something about the interactive dynamic of performance art, a symbiosis of relationship. The artist needs the audience to express his or her art, for the audience is the venue in which art becomes known. And the audience needs the artist to receive the art, to help them feel it, understand it.

Ken Gire writes: "My own understanding is that of a writer, not a theologian. But if faith is the substance of things unseen, maybe we come closer to spiritual things with our imaginations than our intellects. Maybe analysis cannot probe as deeply into such things as can art. If so, the artist, the musician, the writer, may have the upper hand, however feeble, when it comes to such things."[1]

So the world needs the artist, in part to help it interpret, color, redefine, coalesce. And also, sometimes to critique, challenge, and rebuke. It is the obligation of the artist to play this role for the world. The role of the audience, however, is less defined. The audience is anyone who allows himself the possibility of being moved by the artist and his work. Now this definition allows a spectrum of responses, from enjoyment to contempt to indifference. But—and this may come as news to some—we are ultimately not responsible for the response of the audience. We are only responsible for the art that draws that audience and for our role in that dialogue.

Art then is both personal and communal in nature. It is personal in that it is an intimate expression of the artist. And it is communal in that art requires an audience in order for it to be appreciated. The artist and the audience are intricately and inexplicably tied together in an unspoken relationship of expression. As Jeremy Begbie asserts, "Art, as we might say, is inherently dialogical."[2]

It is important for the artist to understand that, in a very real sense, we must be servants to our audience. And this takes many forms. We must not disrespect them with our perceptions of self-importance. We should endeavor to engage, if not entertain, them with our performances. We need to be sensitive to where they are, and meet them there, in order to take them where we want to go. And we serve them by giving them the freedom to have their own opinions of our art apart from us. There is a fine line here, as respecting and being sensitive to our audience does not mean simply catering to them. We are not monkeys on an organ grinder's chain. But as performers, we have obligations to our audience—to be honest, to be gracious, to be invitational, and above all, to be aware of the dialogue inherent in our artistic performances. Remember that we are not just artists, but we all are a part of someone else's audience as well.

> WE GIVE UNDUE POWER TO PEOPLE THAT ONLY GOD SHOULD HAVE—TO GIVE US VALUE AND WORTH.

Some artists have a tendency to treat their audiences with disdain. Miles Davis, the aloof and enigmatic jazz icon, would typically turn his back toward his audience. The punk rock groups of the seventies would treat their audiences with fashionable and nihilistic rudeness. The same is true with strings of artists involved in the modern art movement. But being aloof or snobbish or condescending should not be a part of our role as artists, much less in our role as Christ-followers.

Ironically, I believe that one of the reasons performers treat their audiences badly is because they have an unhealthy need for their audiences' approval. When we are honest with ourselves, we can admit that we crave the acceptance and approval of others. And we artists have learned that we can receive that through our art. David Bayles and Ted Orland, in their book *Art & Fear*, suggest that there is a distinct difference between acceptance and approval. They assert, "Acceptance means having your work counted as the real thing; approval means having people like it."[3] We crave the acceptance of critics and opinion leaders to validate *our work*; we crave the approval of others to validate *us*. And although this is normal for the artist, it is ultimately unhealthy, for we give undue power to people which only God should have—to give us value and worth.

It has taken me a long time to get to the point where I can perform with this type of freedom—passionately attached to the art but graciously detached from the acceptance or rejection of it by the audience. It is something to which I still aspire. But it is a freedom that allows me to truly express myself without guile or hidden agenda or self-deceit.

Now at the risk of sounding Zen pop weird, let me pose the rhetorical question: If the artist needs the audience, does this mean that without the audience, there is no art? Like the tree that falls in the woods, isn't a painting still art, regardless of whether or not someone sees it?

I personally reject this notion. But for different reasons than you might think. In our art, there are always two audiences: one horizontal and one vertical. God, who exists not only in eternity but also in omnipresence, is always an audience for the artist, whether they know it or not. Every word written, every idea birthed, every note played, has been read and seen and heard by our all-knowing God. And for the Christian artist, there should be—must be—a constant awareness aof nd priority to our vertical Audience, not just in our art, but in everything we do. For there is nothing that you have ever done that did not have an Audience of One.

"Where can I go from your Spirit? Where can I flee from your presence? If I go up to the heavens, you are there; if I make my bed in the depths, you are there. If I rise on the wings of the dawn, if I settle on the far side of the sea, even there your hand will guide me, your right hand will hold me fast" (Psalm 139:7–10).

The Christian artist, more deeply than most, should know that we are God's art, cooperating with His Spirit to be an expression of the Master Artist. We must understand that life isn't just about *doing*, but about *being*, and our God is intimately concerned about who we are and who we are becoming. And we must also know that our own artistic expressions are ultimately birthed from His inspiration. For all inspiration ultimately comes from God the Creator, through His Spirit. And we must have the ears to hear His small, still voice. And finally, we must know the heart of God, so that we might put a smile on His face with our artistic expressions. We must strive to use our art in the truest, most free sense, uncluttered by pride and envy and other sins, and simply align with His heart, so that we might live with the purpose that the Westminster Catechism states so eloquently: "Man's chief and highest end is to glorify God, and fully to enjoy him forever."

We exist in these two planes of relationship with both of our audiences. And hence, in our vertical relationship, the artist and our Trinitarian Audience are intricately and inexplicably tied together in an unspoken relationship of expression. This is why art is such a spiritual endeavor. And to understand this as an artist is to know Joy.

I love to play for this Audience of One. The feedback, the immediacy, the intimacy, the freedom. Because the artist needs the Audience to inspire and express and receive. And the Audience desires community with the artist, for He receives joy and glory through it.

And that is the way, I believe, it was intended to be.

A CALL TO ARTISTIC COMMUNITY

The Bible is not primarily a history book or a book of philosophy. It is primarily a book that documents the relationship between God and His people. It is a book of relationships, both vertical and horizontal. It is a book about love—love lost, love found, love triumphant, love calling, love enduring.

In it, God calls us to community. Through trials, misfortunes, sins, and tragedies, the Bible describes the relationships of God's people with one another and with Him. There is never an indication of faith or law or God's will without the context of community to frame it.

There is one community in particular to which I relate. In the Old Testament book of Numbers, God specifically calls out one of the tribes of the Hebrew nation, the descendants of Levi, to be His servants in the tabernacle. God speaks to Moses and calls the tribe of the Levites from the rest of the nation to dedicate them into full-time service. Under the leadership of Aaron and his sons, the Levites become a God-ordained organization of priests, attendants, and artists, including artisans, craftsmen, and musicians.

"Then the Lord spoke to Moses, saying, 'Bring the tribe of Levi near and set them before Aaron the priest, that they may serve him.

They shall perform the duties for him and for the whole congregation before the tent of meeting, to do the service of the tabernacle" (Numbers 3:5–7 NASB).

This was the ultimate gig. They didn't have to grow food or tend sheep or perform many of the other difficult aspects of simply living in ancient times. They could concentrate fully on the duties of being musicians and artists and worship leaders and attendants of the tabernacle. And the other tribes would support them.

Over time—from Moses to David and Solomon—this artistic and priestly organization became the group that oversaw and maintained the temple under Solomon, which ultimately existed as the holy place of community between God and His people.

We need to understand the cultural and historical context of the building of the temple (which is documented in 2 Chronicles 2–4). There had never been a permanent place of worship in the history of the nation Israel until this point. There had never before been an artistic and architectural endeavor this size undertaken by God's chosen people. And never had there been the fullness of God's glory manifested in a man-made creation as this.

In this increased role, God was very specific in the numbers of people used and the various roles they had. The total number of Levites (age thirty and above) who were involved in the temple was 38,000, of which 4,000 were musicians (1 Chronicles 23). These musicians were skilled in the use of cymbals, stringed instruments, and harps (1 Chronicles 25). (Insert your favorite drummer joke here.) And these numbers obscure the larger numbers associated with the families of these adults—including those children and young adults in training—who were set apart by God for these purposes. One can ascertain that they were a highly organized and exceptionally trained group focused on one thing—glorifying the Living God.

Dr. Bruce Leafblad, in his paper "Music, Worship, and the Ministry of the Church," summarizes the relationship of the Levites to God in this way:

> Skill, training, and musical understanding were all important facets that influenced the organization of the Levitical musicians. It is not God's way to ask one to exercise a gift he does not possess or to utilize a talent he does not have. In the divine economy there is a definite place for the exercising of wisdom and reason regarding abilities, talents and similar personal qualities. . . . And in this account God gloriously blesses his people with a marvelous display of his glory in direct affirmation of and response to the obedient carrying out his divine play for the Temple—its facilities, its staff, and its ministry, including the official establishment of the ministry of music.[4]

Here is the point: none of this—the architecture, the statues, the furnishings, the musical instruments, and the music itself—could have happened without a highly organized and committed community. Artists were specifically called by God, endowed with gifts and talents, given a common vision, and unleashed to glorify Him through the communal action of their artistry.

Warren Bennis wrote a fascinating book entitled *Organizing Genius*. In it, he describes the creative collaborations of seven "Great Groups," creative organizations that changed modern history. They include Walt Disney Studios, Apple Computers, Lockheed's Skunk Works, and the Manhattan Project, all examples of great artistic and scientific leapfrogging, of redefinition, of paradigmatic shift. And in it, he espouses the genius of creative collaboration in depth. He mentions Michelangelo as a "classic example":

"In our mind's eye, we see Michelangelo, looking remarkably like Charlton Heston, laboring alone on the scaffolding high above the chapel floor. In fact, thirteen people helped Michelangelo paint the work. Michelangelo was not only an artist, he was, as biographer William E. Wallace points out, the head of a good-sized entrepreneurial enterprise that collaboratively made art that bore his name."[5]

He goes on to describe the synergistic collaboration of the French Impressionists, which included Monet, Degas, Renoir, and Manet, who would paint together, drink together, and philosophize together. They understood that it was in community that something great would happen.

The study of Walt Disney is a fascinating one, in which, driven by an insatiable dream, he single-handedly envisioned and assembled an incredibly talented group of visual artists, painters, writers, and cinematographers. Together, they redefined an art form: the animated film.

THERE WAS A SENSE THAT GOD WAS IN THE ROOM, AND HE WAS UP TO SOMETHING.

Apparently, Disney went so far as to create a college of sorts to teach the craft, even before his first full-length film, *Snow White*, was completed. Such was the power of his vision.

Through a variety of circumstances, I had the privilege of becoming friends with Bob Kilpatrick, songwriter, worship leader, recording artist, and one of the pioneers of contemporary Christian music. He is primarily known as the author of the classic chorus "Lord, Be Glorified." A number of years ago, Bob and I had an idea. We would try to gather the pro and semipro Christian musicians in our area and have a party. There were so many people who knew people who knew people, and we thought it might be good if everyone finally met face-to-face. We called everyone we knew and told them to invite everyone they knew. And for some strange reason, they came. Looking around that evening, I took a mental inventory of the participants: Owners and engineers of some of the area's top recording studios, music and worship pastors from some of the area's most creative churches, well-known Christian musicians and bands. It was such a cool vibe, knowing that God was working through all these talented people to express Himself.

These weren't perfect people. I'm sure there were dysfunctional dynamics in the crowd, some posturing, some pride, some tension, some unspoken sinful thoughts. But there was also a sense that God was in the room, and He was up to something. This meeting turned into a once-a-month gathering, where we would pray for and encourage one another. It also became the catalyst for a lot of bands working with each other, helping each other, instead of competing with one another. One band had a contact with a CD manufacturer and shared it with another. Another band would loan its PA system to another band. One person would open for another, or give him the name of someone who owned a club. There were some elements of community happening, real friendships made, and it was a very cool thing.

In a sense, we were acting like modern Levites, all understanding our place before God and our role in community. All of us helping, encouraging, and edifying the body of Christ outside the bounds of denominationalism and self-interest. And really, shouldn't this be normative? Shouldn't this happen between artists, between bands, between churches?

In the Bible, and in real life, it is clear that we were not intended to live as individuals but within the context of community. And I am convinced that the same is true for artists. Thus, as artists, we have the need to create within the communal context, helping one another, developing our art, and encouraging one another toward art.

THE SHADOW IN OUR HEARTS

For a period in my young adult life, I had a consuming dream. I wanted to be a rock star. In my Walter Mittyesque daydreams, I pictured myself performing cutting-edge but timeless music, with relevant but flippant lyrics, creative but mindless dance grooves, and inventive but totally catchy, hum-in-the-shower melodies. And rock-and-roll babes would flock to me, asking for my autograph, admiring me in my leather pants yet at the same time loving me for my mind.

The rock-and-roll dream was very much a part of my life. It affected how I managed my career, how I spent my time, and even how I saw the world. As a young man, I became an engineer, in part because I wanted to be able to finance my rock-and-roll fantasy. In retrospect, the rock-and-roll dream was a substitute for my secret childhood dream of being a classical pianist, and in a way, it was much more dangerous. It was my unspoken motivation for rehearsing, writing music, playing gigs, getting good. In fact, every musician I encountered, I would subconsciously put into one of three categories: "Not as good as me," "Just as good as me," or "I could play better than him if I worked at it." And it made me work even harder.

ONE OF THE UNSPOKEN IRONIES OF BEING A CHRISTIAN MUSIC ARTIST IS THAT SO MUCH OF THE APPLAUSE IS DIRECTED TOWARD US.

And then, on a seemingly ordinary evening in the warm July of 1985, I discovered a different perspective of the universe. I found a relationship with Jesus Christ. And my outlook on my music—and my life—has never been the same.

I call the rock-and-roll dream dangerous because it was a goal that, in a sense, dominated my life. I had centered my life goals on it; my self-worth was partly derived from it. Yet its attainment would have left me with nothing of any value. It was an illusory, worldly, self-serving goal for which to live one's life. King Solomon, the wisest and richest king of his day, knew this, and he described the attainment of fame and wealth like this: "Smoke, nothing but smoke. . . . There's nothing to anything—it's all smoke" (Ecclesiastes 1:2 THE MESSAGE). And it continues to be dangerous because I will always suffer from bouts of pride and selfishness. I believe it is probably the artist's favorite sin.

And that is the "S" word. Sin. In today's world, it is not very fashionable or enlightened to believe in such an antiquated notion. And yet, sin and its consequences are all around us. And inside of us as well. Sin is real. And sin will kill you.

Art is an expression of the heart. And as such, art is inexplicably tied to our sinful nature in deep and complex ways. The nature of artists is to be competitive, feed ego, seek fame. It was the sin of Lucifer, who was an artist extraordinaire, the "Morning Star." It was the sin of King David, who wrote some of the most beautiful music ever written in his Psalms. It was the sin of countless artists, from prima ballerinas to rap stars, from da Vinci to Sinatra, who proudly crooned, "I did it my way."

We all know the story. Moses is on the mountain representing the people of Israel to God Himself, and Aaron is at base camp leading the people in the creation and worship of a golden calf. Moses gets back from his trip and goes ballistic. For he has seen the very Face of God, and his fellow Israelites are content to worship a shiny metal statue. One of the unspoken ironies of being a Christian music artist is that so much of the applause is directed toward us. Certainly, there is a place for these things, but we must resist the sin of making ourselves "idols."

This is the sin that accompanies fame, the sin of believing the hype that we are more than we are, the sin of craving attention that should be focused on God. For it inflates us, denigrates God, misrepresents the Gospel, and breaks the third commandment. As artists, it is exceedingly difficult to not be lured by the lust for fame, the sin of pride, the need to become a golden calf.

The more subtle form of this is that we begin to act like prima donnas—musicians who don't show up on time, demean other performers, demand more of their own voices in the monitors. Actors who are critical of others but cannot receive constructive criticism themselves. Authors who cannot celebrate the successes of their peers. Artists who forget that their role is actually one of a servant. We betray our pride with such acts and abuse the very nature of the gifts God gives us.

Probably the biggest thing I have learned about myself is how insidious pride can be. Truth be told, there was more wrapped up in my identity as a pastor of a fast-growing church than should have been allowed. But pride can be a very ugly thing. So I learned how to hide it, justify it, live in it, and then take it out and wade in it when no one else was looking.

There is an irony in this. And this will seem obvious after I say it. The role of the artist is to express art. And the better you are, the more your art will move people. But . . . the better you are, the less you seemingly need God to move in you. The best of us have the greatest temptation—to rely on oneself, on one's own talents and skills and charisma. And what an irony, what a waste, when the greatest artists that God produces turn away from Him because of the very gifts He gives them.

But the role of an artist or worship leader in the church, as is the role of pastor or minister, is one of a servant. We exist to serve others, to help them grow and live in the Kingdom, not to simply use them to fulfill our agendas. To bring people to the throne of God, and not stand in the way of it. To put away the sin of pride, the sin of "me." To die to Christ, every single day. And it is this last part that I am still learning.

A. W. Tozer tells a story that goes like this: Jesus fulfilled Scripture when He rode a young donkey into Jerusalem in John 12:12–16. The great crowds came to meet Him, taking palm branches and spreading them out before Him, praising His name, shouting "Hosanna! Hosanna!" The donkey, looking around at the crowd, then thought to himself, "Wow! I must really be great!" In the grand scheme of things, we're just the donkey. We need to remember that.

THE INSTITUTION OF THE CHURCH, WHICH HISTORI-CALLY HAS A RICH AND FULL TRADITION IN THE ARTS, OFTEN DOES NOT KNOW HOW TO EMBRACE THE ARTIST.

The carnal nature toward self that artists have is contrary to our basic need and calling toward community. For it alienates us from one another and from God. It turns us into competitors instead of compatriots. It pushes us into our own internal worlds and away from one another.

It is this carnal nature of the artist that has historically made artists suspect to the church. In the context of the illiterate laity that formed the church of the Middle Ages, it was common to use non-written art forms to tell the Gospel story. Thus, symbolism abounded—a red cloth on the altar signified Jesus' blood, the gothic arches of the cathedral signified the loftiness of heaven, the pointy hats of the bishops signified the tongues of fire that appeared above everyone's heads on the day of Pentecost. And so on. Painters and sculptors were used extensively, not only to create sacred space but also to tell the story to the illiterate congregation. And there were pageants, Easter's Holy Week and Advent's Christmas, to celebrate and exposit the birth of Christ and His death and resurrection.

But somewhere in there, the artists took over. The medium gradually became more important than the message. The show became more important than the celebration. And in response to all of that, art and beauty were kicked out of the church.

Today, art and beauty are regularly celebrated in the secular world. The Grammys, the Oscars, the People's Choice Awards, the 50 Most Beautiful People. The world uses art to tell its stories, entertain the masses, sell soft drinks, promote its politics. And the church largely sits on the outside, dwelling in a din of artistic mediocrity. Ironically, the institution of the church, which historically has a rich and full tradition in the arts, often does not know how to embrace artists, teaching them the noble and God-glorifying calling that they have.

But the calling of the church, if it is to seek fullness of Christian community, should be to seek a place where artists are encouraged, discipled, held accountable, and applauded for their role in the church. And in spite of the sinful nature of artists, allow them the opportunity to find their place, use their voices, answer their callings—all within the context of the church, the body of Christ.

Fortunately for me, I died to my rock-and-roll dream. I realized that God didn't want me to be that rock star and live in that world. No leather pants, no MTV, no screaming guitars or jumping on a grand piano, no rock-and-roll babes. That dream would have fed a very stubborn, incredibly large and ugly ego inside of me. Simply put, God didn't want me to be the center of my life. He wanted to be it instead. So I died. And every day, I must die again.

I don't have this all figured out. I can't say that I'm in a church where all of this is happening. But I do feel that the church must be a place where the world sees God—in our speech, in our actions, in our passion, and in our art. We need more Christian artists who die to themselves. And we need more churches who embrace them.

REFLECTIONS OF THE FALSE SELF

At this point, I feel compelled—for the sake of authenticity—to share a little of the other side of myself. It's obvious that I haven't conquered the sins of my life, or that I don't have it all together. On the contrary, as I become more mature in my faith, I am becoming more acutely aware of my own sinfulness and the baggage associated with it.

I mentioned earlier that my piano playing, and my art in general, became a way that I gave myself worth and gave form to my self-identity. I think it began with me coping with my own insecurities, as a nearsighted, socially challenged, non-athletic, dumpy Filipino kid who lived on the wrong side of town. I was the kid who was always picked last on the playground, the kid in class commonly referred to as "four eyes," the kid who was painfully shy around girls. And although my parents loved me unconditionally and my friends were loyal and true, I had a less-than-ideal home life and a childhood that was a struggle. I remember vividly an episode in third grade: I wet my pants during class from my own nervousness and insecurity. I can still remember hearing the laughter from the other children, as the puddle beneath my seat grew larger and more incriminating.

> I WAS KNOWN AS THE SMART ONE, THE TALENTED ONE, AND I CLUNG TO THESE LABELS AND MADE THEM PART OF MY IDENTITY.

But I excelled in academics and music, and I began to build my identity around these socially accepted roles. I became the brightest kid in every class. I was accelerated one year in grade school. I became first chair in all the school bands and eventually went on to make the

All-State Honor band. I played keyboards in the school stage band and wrote music for talent nights. I eventually became valedictorian of my high school. Now there is more than a bit of image management that goes on when you reach the age of self-examination, and I was no exception. I was known as the smart one, the talented one, and I clung to these labels and made them part of my identity.

Old habits are hard to break. By the time I was a young adult, I was still doing no small amount of image management, exuding the vibe of an up-and-coming professional who was cool enough to play in bar bands after hours. Frankly, I liked this part of who I was, and not the part of me who still felt like that short, insecure Filipino kid in the glasses. Now, one of the aspects of image management is to actually believe you are who you pretend to be. It is a part of the psychological mechanism. So I bought into my own lies, and became quietly prideful of my achievements and my talents and my social standing and my financial status.

I am not alone in this web of self-deception. We artists have a natural tendency to want to believe the lie that we are more than simply the artist that God made us to be. We tend to create and embrace a false sense of self, choosing to believe the inflated hype that makes us more important than we really are. We justify our sins, our negative predispositions, our vices, in light of this inflated self. And we hide behind it, for if the truth were known, we are all bathed in a complex maze of insecurity and doubt and dysfunction and neediness, like layers of shadows in our hearts. And for many of us, the shadow is too dark for us to see, too dark to even fathom or recognize.

I REMEMBER PREACHING ON THE SIN OF PRIDE ONCE. I THOUGHT I DID GREAT.

When I became a Christ-follower as an adult, things started to turn upside down. God began the process of stripping my false self away, and I began to learn for the first time how to become the person God intended me to be. Deep down, I felt like I was now living an intentionally godly life. But even in my humility, there was pride. For while we are no longer subject to our sin nature, it is with us just the same.

Please don't get me wrong. I wasn't a poster child for split personality disorder. I genuinely cared for people, loved my family and friends, had high moral integrity, and wanted to follow Jesus. But there were elements of my pride and insecurity and self-centeredness that were buried within me. They were deeper than I realized. And I didn't have the emotional IQ then to see it, much less dismantle it.

In the midst of all of this, I left my career in aerospace for a ministry position in a church. Does one see the irony in being complimented for being a good worship leader? Or for having some amount of hidden pride for preaching a great sermon? Or being praised for being a pastor who models humility? The truth is that I personally took way too much credit for the successes of our ministry. I came to believe, in an unstated way, that my omni-competence was a major cause of our success. Without knowing it at the time, I was motivated as much to build my own reputation as I was to build up the church. And, just as I did as a child, I built my identity around my position as a talented, hip, musical pastor at a hot, new, fast-growing church. I became rather puffed up in my humility, actually. And I hid it really well.

I remember preaching on the sin of pride once. I thought I did great.

There is an inherent complicity with being associated with success, even success in ministry. And I was sucked in, just like everyone else. Every song I performed or wrote, every drama script I authored, every sermon I preached, every group I led, had some small and

unnoticed attachment to my self-image. I believed, in a deeply sinis-
ter and hidden way, that my identity was rooted in the successes of my
ministry and my art. In essence, I believed that God couldn't really
do all this without me. He was lucky to have me, really. And this attitude only served to feed my false self more.

I believe that the false self is extremely prevalent in the church.
For one of the inadvertent and unstated values in a church is that
everyone is supposed to have their act together, to have strong spiritual muscles, to walk the walk, to never sin. And for some churches,
this unintended value is held so high that it becomes necessary for
people to create false selves, in order to measure up to standards. So instead of being real with their feelings, their insecurities, their sins,
they fake it. They pretend everything is fine, they speak religious talk,
they say all the right prayers, act the right way, and go to all the right
events. And this creates another danger—of creating a religiosity that
is mistaken for real Christianity. When that happens, people can never
be truly authentic, never truly self-aware, never truly broken before
God. Churches, even the most intentionally authentic ones, can be
breeding grounds for image management.

This intricate web of persona is extremely common for the artist,
who by nature has a public stage persona apart from their normal persona. I believe artists act this way—in all of life—more than they care
to admit. There are complex and deeply personal reasons why we are
drawn to the applause of a crowd, and the need for fame and fortune.
And what many of us do is create a false self, an outer persona that we
can hide behind and spin to suit us. I would go so far to say that almost
every talented artist has a problem in this area, and those who don't
are either not self-aware or in denial.

The bottom line of living this way is that one is never truly
transformed. We simply conform to the trappings of religiosity, spend-

ing an inordinate amount of time and energy managing our image, trying to impress or fit in, stuffing away our insecurities and insufficiencies and emotional infirmities. But in order to truly be transformed, to be the person God intended us to be, we must be willing to let go of who we pretend to be, who we want people to think we are, and even who we actually think we are but are not. And this can be a painful process.

Jesus understood the trappings of religiosity, the heavy burdens it imposed upon people, and how image management and false self are contrary to the ways of His Father. Sympathetically and in loving kindness, He invites us to another way:

> *Are you tired? Worn out? Burned out on religion? Come to me. Get away with me and you'll recover your life. I'll show you how to take a real rest. Walk with me and work with me—watch how I do it. Learn the unforced rhythms of grace. I won't lay anything heavy or ill-fitting on you. Keep company with me and you'll learn to live freely and lightly. (Matthew 11:28–30 THE MESSAGE)*

God has a way of weeding these things out of one's life. In these recent years, God has taken me on a circuitous route, away from "success," away from the spotlight of ministry, and deepened the process of stripping away the false self. He has taken away some of the artificial props of my life, and put me in positions where I had to deal with my own weaknesses and foibles. Frankly, it has not been an easy thing. But through it all, I am understanding in deeper and deeper ways that God's agenda must supersede mine. I am learning more and more to believe that I am doing the most important thing in the world, but I am not important because I am doing it. I am realizing that I can be a part of making great music while not believing that I am so great. I am experiencing more and more God's infinite love for me, and how His grace forgives every sin. In greater measure, I am placing my identity in Christ alone.

And through all of that, I know more and more each day that God loves the insecure, piano-playing Filipino kid with the glasses who still lives inside of me.

PLEASE DON'T LET ME
BE MISUNDERSTOOD

When I came to a saving relationship with Jesus Christ, the last part of me to be saved was the part that loved music. Let me explain.

The modern American Christian subculture was in its adolescence in the summer of 1985, when I first came to be a Christ-follower.[6] And I was interested in knowing what kind of music was out there. Unfortunately, there wasn't much. I remember going to the local Christian bookstore and listening to the pabulum that was then Contemporary Christian Music (also known as CCM). Some of it sounded like soft rock from the early seventies, with lyrics that contained a lot of clichés and bad poetry (Hey, let's rhyme "love" with "above"!). Tame worship music that sometimes sounded like so many children's nursery rhymes. No jazz, no edgy rock, few truly unique musical statements. Outside of some notable exceptions, the state of the genre left me somewhat wanting. And stylistically, there also seemed to be a very narrow band of acceptability, with most of the music being derivative of the secular market. And I bought into that as the norm.

So it was with some reluctance that I came to Christ. Not that I didn't want God's gift of grace, or His healing, or His acceptance, or an intimate relationship with Him. I definitely wanted all of those things. I just didn't want His music.

Although things have gotten considerably better (and considerably worse) for CCM, I believe there is still a great relational path that must be forged between the artist and the local church. Certainly even today, the artist is looked upon with some disdain (at worst) and misunderstanding (at best) by the modern Protestant church. Or for those few on the A-list, an extremely unhealthy hero worship can result (that helps neither the artist nor the church). And speaking in generalities, artists—especially photographers, dancers, sculptors, and others whose art forms don't directly translate to a typical church service—feel like there is no place for them within the church. So they seek to find their venues for expression outside the church walls, in the larger marketplace of the world. Why is this the case? For right or wrong, I offer a few reasons from the standpoint of the church.

Artists are weird. They often speak a different language, seemingly have a different set of values, and see the world in a different way. Oftentimes, their hair is too long or too short, they wear earrings and have body piercings, and they sport tattoos in unusual places. They just don't quite look like the rest of us. They are often on the fringe of acceptability, and just as often, they choose to live there.

Artists are difficult to control. They have artistic visions and values that often run at odds with the vision and values of the local church. They sometimes see requests to conform to the church vision and values as areas of compromise or toning down their art. Some have melancholy personalities and ulterior motives, and are somewhat self-absorbed (usually masking some area of insecurity). Many artists don't know how to be team players, either to take direction or to give it. In short, artists can be a pain in the rear at times.

Artists are needy people. Their art comes from their brokenness, from their own personal journeys toward wholeness. But that also means that the artist needs lots of nurturing, discipline, encouragement. And it seems like there isn't enough time in the day for some of these people. It takes a lot of time to hold an artist accountable, to continue to affirm and instruct, to teach them their very special role in the church. But the artist, in their pride, sometimes does not see the necessity for accountability and discipleship in their journey. Although they crave feedback and affirmation, they often take criticism poorly. So the artist will often get their feelings hurt, or they will feel misunderstood, and they martyr themselves to justify their self-perceptions. (I'll be covering this in more depth in chapter 5.)

Art can be controversial, and the nature of churches is to try to avoid controversy. Because the band of acceptability in the church is often a narrow one, many art forms, if they are to be used in any substantive way in a church setting, must be explained. And it is difficult to have to explain art in the local church when many churches do not have a well-formed theology of art or an artistically driven culture. I have heard many stories from worship and arts pastors who tried to introduce dance or painting or other art forms into their churches, and were met by indifference or hostility. And I remember playing with my jazz group in a traditional church setting and actually having groups of people in the audience turn their seats to deliberately put their backs toward us.

Art in the church is all too often judged solely for its spirituality and not its artistry. This has been the case for so long that many churched people don't know good art from bad. This is especially true in the churches where Aunt Martha is allowed to sing, because she's Aunt Martha (not that there's anything wrong with that!). If the church doesn't have artistry as a fundamental value, it will have a hard time understanding the place of art in the church. So while it is true that we are born with a God-given aesthetic, the church oftentimes is not.

Conversely, *the artist in the church is all too often judged solely for his artistry and not his spirituality.* I admit to having made this mistake early in my ministry career, where I allowed incredible musicians to take the stage, knowing that their walks were not all that consistent. The music was great, but the spiritual integrity of the music was not.

But for all the eccentricities, the misunderstandings, the controversies, the offenses—the messiness—the Christ-following artist is still a part of the universal church, a part of the body. And the church needs the artist, just as the artist needs the church. For we are all a part of the body together, and we are only complete when we live and function and love together. Ken Gire writes, "We learn from the artists, from those who work in paint or words, or musical notes, from those who have eyes that see and ears that hear and hearts that feel deeply and passionately about all that is sacred and dear to God."[7]

> THE PART OF ME THAT LOVED MUSIC WAS THE LAST PART OF ME TO BE SAVED.

I have seen both sides of all of these aspects of the messiness, being an artist by design and a pastor by calling. I have made many of the mistakes too. But I believe that the calling of the church as it relates to the artist must be threefold: One, to be a *venue* for the art (a place, a way, and a time); two, to be a biblical *community* with the artist (offering friendship, encouragement, training, and discipleship); and three, to be an *audience* for the artist, for the church needs artists to fulfill their God-given roles in the body of Christ, to reflect, to interpret, to express, and to inspire.

I don't pretend to know all the answers. And there is an inherent complexity to creating an artistic culture within the church. For we are messy people. But I believe that it is necessary to live in the messiness, if we are to become the fully formed church God intended us to be.

I mentioned at the beginning of this section that the part of me that loved music was the last part of me to be saved. It has been a circuitous path that has led me to believe that it is music that continues to "save" me. In a way, it is music that is one of my primary means to seek relationship with God. And it is the way that God continues to draw me and use me still.

MINISTRY LESSONS LEARNED

There is no little irony in the fact that I found myself, in the fall of 1990, quitting my engineering job in a local aerospace company to become the arts and worship pastor for my church. The pudgy Filipino kid with glasses who wanted to be a concert pianist and later a rock star, a former Catholic who rejected the religion of his youth and became an intellectual humanist, the fast-tracked young buck with the MBA. But deep in my soul, I wanted my life to matter. I wanted to make a difference. An eternal difference. And that desire led me down this path.

At the time, I had been a regular volunteer on our church's worship team, and my wife and I were three years into our marriage—with a toddler, a brand-new baby, a minivan, and a mortgage payment. Our church was searching for a minister of worship, and the process had been going on for a while. Though we experienced a parade of well-meaning, Christ-loving, Bible-college graduates, there just didn't seem to be any candidates who were a good fit for our church's renegade mentality. I had thrown myself into my career, and was working my way into management. After a two-year management training program, I had just been given a raise and a promotion, and I was reporting directly to one of the vice presidents of the company. But there was an increasing discontentedness with my life that I couldn't shake.

One day, I came home from work and half-joked to my wife Debbie, "What if I applied for the worship position at church?" I expected Debbie to laugh, but she took me very seriously. She replied, "Honey, if you feel that way, then we should pray about it." She had called my bluff. And so we prayed. Prayed hard.

Two weeks later, we found ourselves having a meeting with our senior pastor and the head of our elder board. We were trying to figure out what the minimum amount was they could pay me so I could continue to keep my house. A month after that, I found myself in the office of my vice president, telling him I wanted to work for God instead. By October of 1990, I was working full-time as the minister of worship for Oak Hills Church in Folsom, California.

That's when God really started making things interesting. Our church of about 200 people had purposed ourselves to reach our area, and was prepared to unleash whatever resources were necessary to do so. My hiring was key to this vision for ministry. We began to reorient the entire church around a style of ministry called "seeker-targeted," which is a philosophy of outreach using highly charged and arts-oriented weekend services to share the Gospel. Based on the pioneering work of Willow Creek Community Church in the Chicago area, we were intent on doing a West Coast version of Willow, to capture our community for Jesus Christ.

We began an outreach service in early 1991, and we soon were bringing in 150 people on a Saturday night, in addition to our regular Sunday afternoon worship service. When we finally got onto some property of our own and began services on Sunday morning (we hadn't had a Sunday morning service in three years), we immediately grew to 500 weekend attendance. A year later, we were at 650. A year after that, we were at 800. Soon after, we had become a church of over 1,200 weekend attendance, and we were running five services a week in our tiny building. And by the year 2000, when we were able to build and move into our first permanent building, a performing arts auditorium with adjacent classrooms, we were threatening the 2,000 mark.

One of the keys to this growth was our weekend services, called "seeker" services, which were designed primarily for those checking out the Christian faith. We had established an arts community of almost a hundred people to support this seeker machine: drama team, seeker bands, worship teams, a planning team, a communications team, and a large technical team. We even had a recording studio and a publishing ministry. I was creating and performing some of the best music and drama of my life—and we were having a blast doing it.

> BECAUSE GOD IS OUR AUDIENCE, ART CAN ALSO BE AN "END" IN ITSELF.

Looking back in retrospect, I see myself in those years, as blessed as they were, as being somewhat superficial. For one thing, I think my theology and philosophy of ministry had some growing up to do. I also believe that God still needed to teach me in deeper ways what is the calling of the pastor, what is the heart that must beat within. And I needed to learn in more profound and desperate ways to rely more on God and His power than on my own talents and abilities.

Years have allowed me a glimpse of some lessons learned, things from my history that I would not want to repeat, but I am grateful to have learned. I list some of them here below:

An end unto itself. In the previous chapter (where I quote Francis Schaeffer), we discussed the contrasting ideas of art being a vehicle for a message versus art being simply an expression of our story, and how it relates to our individual art. This concept also applies to the local church. In these recent times, the trend in the church is to use the arts as a means to an end, e.g., art as a vehicle for worship or art as a means of outreach and evangelism. It is this philosophy that drove my church in the early days. In crass terms, we put on a show of sorts, a horizontally designed presentation using complementary artistic elements all purposefully embedded with a Gospel theme. We also used music as our primary means of worship, seeing worship as a set of songs strung together during our worship service.

I am beginning to believe that art is not simply a means to an end, but because God is our Audience, art can also be an "end" in itself. And this holds true for the church as well as the individual. So the church becomes an advocate for art—even if it has no agenda. My church now has an ongoing art gallery that has no other purpose than to allow visual artists and poets an opportunity to share their stories with others through their art. We have an ongoing café venue for musical artists to share their music. We have partnered with a local professional theatre company whose goal is not to preach, but to simply present redemptive, quality drama. We've opened up our facility and resources to the city's symphony orchestras, knowing that God just loves great music. In all of these examples, art is simply an expression of the human condition, the human story, not a vehicle for a message or a specific means of evangelism.

Let me give you one final example of this. Not long ago, my church began to re-envision the architecture for our campus. Our original building was designed under certain criteria: multipurpose, utilitarian, non-obtrusive, maximum occupancy, high functionality. The main auditorium was designed to be a performing arts venue, with extensive catwalks and lighting, multimedia, and a honking-great sound system, all serving a large stage. Essentially, it was a box, resembling a business park or an upscale warehouse. But although the auditorium and campus had served us well, the architecture never truly conveyed a sense of the mystery and presence of God.

We had been debating this for quite some time before it hit me one day: architecture is an art. And we had been operating under the paradigm that art was a means to an end. So when we designed the campus, we were operating under the assumption that the building was a means for ministry, a means for communicating the Gospel, for gathering, for giving religious instruction, for putting on events.

And I think this is why we felt something was intrinsically wrong about our campus: we were beginning to see art under the paradigm that art is not merely a vehicle to communicate our faith, but is a direct expression of our faith. Because if architecture is art, then the art of our building should communicate what we believe about God— that He is grace-filled, that He invites people to live in His Kingdom, that He dwells among us, that life with Him is far more glorious and deep and astounding than life without Him. So we began using words like *transcendence, aesthetics, sacredness, hospitality, artistry*. We began envisioning a campus with areas for conversation, contemplation, prayer, worship, and art. The irony is, what we are painting with words is more like a cathedral or a sanctuary, in the most literal sense of the words. We are envisioning a reflection of the presence of God, played out in brick and mortar. One might think that we are embracing some elements of trendy ancient-future postmodernity. But we aren't. I think what is happening more so is that we are stripping ourselves of our modernity, of the frames of linearity and pragmatism and functionality that sometimes imprison us. And allowing the art of our building to reflect our faith.

Being redemptive in our art. Much is said these days about the phrase "redeeming the arts," which is fashionably used in evangelical circles. I have used the term many times myself. One obvious implication of the term is that there must be something wrong with art, particularly art in the world, and that it must be redeemed, i.e., it falls short of the glory of God and must be saved. Certainly it is true that much of art is spiritually skewed, astray of God's intention, and even ungodly and immoral. But of course, art is by nature spiritually non-living, more a function of the expression of the artist and the interpretation of the audience, so in a sense, I don't think the phrase quite captures what it intends to say. For it is not the *art* that needs redemption; it is the *artist*.

WE TELL A GRAND STORY. AND IT NEEDS TO BE TOLD.

It may be more true to say that we are called to be *redemptive in our art*. In other words, we cooperate with the Holy Spirit, moving toward greater Christlikeness, bearing the image of the Creator. And in our redemption, we create art that expresses our redemptive worldview, our ongoing sanctification, our personal narrative. There is a sacredness in the act of creating art that reflects this sacred redemption.

And it is the better way, really. Because it frees us from having to be so "Christian" in our approach to art (for we must avoid creating shallow and naive expressions). Also, it frees us from the prevalent idea that the sole effort of Christian art is as a means toward evangelism. We can simply be real about the human condition and our redeemed humanity. We can seek to express the total expression of man, through the eyes of the Christ-follower. And if we are to reclaim anything, it will be through a cultivation of the arts that moves, compels, relates, transcends. For we tell a grand story. And it needs to be told.

Living with an immanent God. Virtually all of us as Christians give theological assent to the *theory* of God's omnipresent and omnipotent nature. But in most churches, practicing the real and immanent presence of God during the worship service is a bit of a foreign concept. Yet the worship experience is only as good as our ability to practice a practical immanence in worship, to be cognizant of *God in the room* and know that He pervades and sustains the universe. We must learn to respect God's presence by giving Him first place in the service, to try to see Him in the mind's eye in everything done during the service, and to worship as if He were really there. Because He is.

This has practical implications. We design the worship not primarily for the congregation, but for God (we do design the worship, however, so that the congregation can sing for God). We look to God for inspiration in the planning of the services, knowing that He is not only the recipient of worship but the initiator of it as well. We talk more to God than to people during the worship service, and generally try to have a vertical orientation in our souls. We also try to model and practice and teach an attitude of worship during the rehearsal, knowing *Emmanuel*, God Is With Us. And I personally try to have the heart of Isaiah before I take the stage, to know that I am not worthy to be there, but for the grace and calling of God.[8]

> WHAT I SLOWLY CAME TO LEARN OVER TIME WAS THAT THE *PRODUCT* OF MY MINISTRY WAS THE SPIRITUAL HEALTH OF THE PEOPLE IN MY MINISTRY.

The fact of God's immanence carries other implications for our lives and worship. If He is truly pervasive in our universe, truly the sustainer of all things, and if He is truly personal in that pervasiveness, one can recognize the potential of sacredness in every moment. Every act of the self and every act of the church—from celebration to mourning, from excitement to the mundane—has the potential for the sacred. To live in the presence of a benevolent and personal and immanent God is to realize that the act of creating, the act of community, the act of running a church, and even the act of living are sacred things.

The true product of ministry. The church commonly considers the product of the artist to be his or her art. And in my early days, I considered the product of my ministry to be the artistic performance, what happened on the stage. What I slowly came to learn over time was that the *product* of my ministry was the spiritual health of the people in my ministry. Their lives were the true measure of my success as a creative arts pastor. In other words, the true product of ministry is not what we do, but instead who we are becoming. And I feel that, somewhere on the edge of eternity, I will be held accountable for such things. The art that we perform and display is then the *by-product* of these people's lives growing in Christ. I needed to learn to respect the greater Art of the Artist, which is His church.

This manifests itself in many ways: from who I put on stage, to how I treat and love people, to how I run a rehearsal, to what I teach and value and model, to how I deal with conflict, to what I prioritize in my ministry. I began to see my calling as that of a pastor of people, ingrained with a God-given artistry, and it was my role to help them grow both as artists and as Christ-followers. Whatever happened on stage had to flow out of that.

I was approached by a member of the choir once. His kind complaint was that I was spending too much time teaching them about worship, instead of singing. His argument was that we really needed the practice and that our time was too valuable to waste by not singing. My kind reply to him was that the product of our ministry as a choir was not the singing or the performance, but rather in how we align our hearts to God, and then respond to Him in our singing in worship. Without our alignment, all the practice in the world would not make us a better worship choir.

The conclusion of my story is more complicated. After all of the growth, the church leadership began to recognize a new calling away from seeker-style ministry and began to reorient itself—philosophically, theologically, and ministry-wise—around the goal of spiritual formation. And I moved to British Columbia for a time, to use my gifts in a Canadian context, and to allow God to use me and grow me there. Due in large part to our shift, the church shrank drastically, below 1,500, then below 1,000, then below 800. The arts—and the arts community—fell upon hard times. It was with trepidation that I reentered this scenario. But I love the church. And I am certain of my call to it.

> IT WAS INTERESTING TO SEE THE CONGREGATION, WITH A LARGE PORTION OF THEM SMILING AND SINGING LOUDLY, AND ANOTHER PORTION STARING, ARMS FOLDED.

It has been quite an adventure. And the true irony is that in my quest to give up my dreams and follow God, He gave me the desires of my heart. In a sense, I am a full-time musician. I get to be creative. I get to work with all sorts of artists, encouraging them to a larger vision. It is true: to find one's life, one must first lose it.

One thing is certain. I intend not to make the same mistakes again. With any luck at all, I'll make all new ones.

THE GREATEST OF THESE

It was the spring of 2002, and I was a pastoral candidate to a church in British Columbia, Canada. Now, seeking God's calling for a pastor is often a difficult thing, because it requires not only the discernment of God's will, but the discernment of man's politics. I had been in contact with about a dozen churches on the West Coast and had settled on two. There was something about this particular church, for all its unique challenges, and I couldn't shake the fact that I felt

God's still, small tug upon me. I felt that God had uniquely qualified me to help this church, in terms of my passion for worship and the arts, and my increased desire to be used as a pastor. And I felt an unexpected warmth from her people, like the first sunny spring day after a long cold winter. I felt hopeful for them. So my wife and I decided to officially candidate.

Among its dysfunctions (and all churches have them!) was the issue of worship style. There were two polarized and lively camps in the church, spreading themselves widely upon the contemporary versus traditional continuum. I became convinced that the only way to solve this was to teach and model true worship, which was the real issue underlying their disagreements. For I believed that they had mistaken the *style* of worship, which is negotiable, for the *heart* of worship, which is really nonnegotiable and essential to the Christ-following church.

During my candidacy, I was asked to lead worship during a church service. And I did. I designed a worship set at the beginning of the service themed around loving God, and really, it was pretty tame stylistically. I had even taken my earring out during the interview, so as not to offend the older generations. But I was true to the integrity of the songs, and I tried to lead them with authenticity and passion and meaning. It was interesting to see the congregation, with a large portion of them smiling and singing loudly, and another portion staring, arms folded.

Afterward, I was in the church lobby when a tall, older gentleman stopped me. Finger wagging, brows crossed, his face in mine, he began to berate me, criticizing my singing, my worship leading, my song selection, even my faith. A fire blazed in his eyes as he began to lecture me, accuse me, admonish me, even hurt me. I felt as if he was trying to undermine everything I believed and felt about worship.

As I listened to him intently in that moment—my blood pressure rising and anger beginning to boil over inside of me—I realized that I had a choice to make. I could have fought back, thrown Bible verses at him, tried to expose his flawed dogma, and won the argument. I could have walked away from the conversation, walked away from the entire church for that matter. A church full of these guys? Who would want that kind of headache anyway? Or a third option: I could choose to love him. So this is what I did.

After he had finished his tirade, I asked him about what was really behind his words. I told him that there had to be some deeper hurt hidden in his soul for him to act that way in a church. I asked him to try to explain where that hurt came from and how long he had been holding on to it. This was a difficult question for him to answer, because I honestly think that he had never thought about it. After his response, I explained in love that this was a difficult situation because the church was moving in this direction in worship, whether or not I was coming on staff. And it wasn't healthy for him to hold on to the bitterness, hold on to whatever pain was driving him. The choices, while difficult, were easy to list: he had to let it go and give it to God, or move to another church. And then I prayed for him.

After our discussion, he actually thanked me. He assured me that it wasn't personal (although I believe he intended it to be so). And he left graciously.

Now, there isn't a happy ending to this story. I can't tell you that I won him over with a gentle Christlike manner or a Mother Teresa smile. The man continued to be a destructive force in the church until he left (when he became a destructive force at another church). He just had too much baggage, I suppose. That's a reality of ministry. And there are others. I have met the closed-minded. The prejudiced. The egotistical. The gossipers. The hypocrites. The legalists. The dogmatics.

The sinners. They are all around us. They *are* us.

The apostle Paul has a few words for us here. In his first letter to the Corinthians, he warns that even if one could speak in tongues, or prophesy great things, or have great wisdom or knowledge, or feed the poor, or become martyred—he would have nothing if he did not have love. For love was the most important thing.

At the expense of a few liberties, let me parphrase Paul for the artist:

"If I can sing like a Grammy-winning artist and have the voice of an angel, but have not love, I am only a resounding gong or a clanging cymbal. If I can pen great books or compose great sonnets that can move mountains, but have not love, I am nothing. If I can dance with the grace of a prima donna, or headline on a Broadway stage or shred the guitar like a rock-and-roll god, but have not love, I gain nothing. Love is patient, love is kind. It does not envy, it does not boast, it is not proud. It is not rude, it is not self-seeking, it is not easily angered, it keeps no record of wrongs. Love does not delight in evil but rejoices with the truth. It always protects, always trusts, always hopes, always perseveres. Love never fails" (1 Corinthians 13:1–8a ARV—Artist Revised Version).

For those of us who are artists, there is a lesson to be learned here. For at some point in our walk, we will be hurt, or be betrayed, or disagree with something or someone. We will feel misunderstood, wronged, prejudged, unappreciated. It is an inevitable risk when one lives in community, when one lives authentically. And you'll want to walk, give up, take your ball and go home. But that is exactly what the Enemy wants you to do.

Your response, in these times of trepidation, should not be to walk or get angry, or become defensive. Your response should be to choose to love the church. Love the church in the same way that Christ demonstrated His love for her. Love the church for all her imperfections and misgivings. Love the church, because it is the right thing to do. Love the church, because God loves her.

Vincent Van Gogh once said, "The more I think it over, the more I feel there is nothing more truly artistic than to love people."[9]

There are many, some of whom are otherwise mature Christians, who never truly understand this, much less model it. So when the church is faced with a crisis, its natural inclination is to criticize, to find the fault, to take sides, and to eventually leave. But that is not what the church is called to do. We are called to love one another.

Paul stated that "Christ loved the church and gave himself up for her." And then Paul called it a "profound mystery" (Ephesians 5:25, 32). Now by definition, we can't fully understand this. But we know that this love revolves around Christ and His grace toward us. There are three mysteries I have experienced in my own ministry:

- The church is full of sinners. And Christ redeems her.
- The church is the hope of the world. And Christ uses her.
- The church is the bride of Christ. And Christ loves her.

Jesus Christ loved the church with a profound, life-changing, selfless love. As artists, we must do the same. We must love the sinners. We must become the hope of the world. We must yield to the Redeemer and become redeemed. For the artist is a reflection of Christ in the church, whom our God uses to enlighten, indwell, and inspire. But we can do nothing and we will be nothing, if we have not love.

Early in my ministry at my British Columbia church, I met John (not his real name), the elderly father of one of the adult guitar players on the worship team. Older and traditional, John soon let me know that he didn't like the styles of music I was selecting, nor the passion in which I led it. And he was quick with the occasional underhanded, sarcastic comment whenever he was within earshot of me. I never defended myself or fought back (although I wanted to), but I did think it odd that his son was a soft-spoken, big-hearted, distortion-playing electric guitarist my age who apparently had big hair back in the day. Shortly after coming on staff, I was fortunate to recruit his young adult son (John's grandson) to the team to play drums as well. I always try to assign family members to the same worship team (e.g., husbands and wives, fathers and sons), and it was so cool to see the two of them on stage, smiles on their faces, playing for the Lord together.

In that first year of ministry, we had a healing service, where the latter part of the service was devoted to people who needed physical, emotional, or spiritual healing. I, along with the senior pastor and other elders, was assigned to pray for and anoint people who came forward. Things were going well through this portion of the service, when John, by chance, came forward for prayer for a physical ailment and was sent to me. I heard his petitions, prayed for him, and anointed his forehead with oil, before sending him back to his seat. It was an uneventful episode that I forgot until months later.

During a time of quiet reflection and prayer, John came forward onto the stage, made a beeline for me while I was playing the piano, and stopped me in mid-song. Tears in his eyes, he confessed his bitterness toward me, my ministry, and my music. And then he asked for my forgiveness. I was so blown away by his gesture that I was suddenly speechless. Not knowing what to do, I did what my heart required: I hugged him. Amongst the tears of that hug, we exchanged forgiveness and redemption. Wrapped in the gesture of that moment was some baggage that John shed, unspoken carry-ons of intergenerational healing and unrequited bitterness and things only known by God.

And God gave me the incredible privilege of experiencing that, through His love.

"And now these three remain: faith, hope and love. But the greatest of these is love" (1 Corinthians 13:13).

• • •

Summary

Some types of wisdom, you learn. Other types you live. This last chapter was probably more the latter for me. The following is a summary of the thoughts from this chapter, The Artist in Community:

- ֍ Art is by nature both personal and communal. It is personal in that it is an expression of the individual. It is communal in that art requires an audience. For the Christ-following artist, we know we have two audiences, both horizontal and vertical, and our art exists for both these audiences (Psalm 11:4).

- ֍ God calls us to community (Acts 2:42–47). We were not intended to live as individual artists but within the context of life with others (eg., 2 Chronicles 34:12). Thus, as artists, we have the need to create within the context of community, helping one another, developing our art, and encouraging one another toward God-honoring art (Philippians 2:1–4).

- ֍ Since our art is a human expression, then it is inextricably tied to our sin nature, in deep and complex ways (Romans 7:14–24). The nature of artists is to be competitive, feed ego, seek fame, and be driven by pride. This carnal nature is contrary to our basic need for and calling toward being known in community.

- ֍ For many reasons (public persona, ego, insecurity), the artist is susceptible to creating and embracing a false self. We must be critically self-aware in order to not wear the heavy burden of living a disingenuous life (Matthew 11:28–30).

- ֍ The calling of the church, if it is to seek fullness of Christian community, should be to be a place where artists are encouraged, nurtured, discipled, held accountable, and applauded for their role in the church (Ephesians 2:19–22). Thus, the calling of the church as it relates to art is to be: a *venue* for the art (a place, a way, a time); a biblical *community* with the artist (offering friendship, encouragement, training, and discipleship); and an *audience* for the artist.

§ Our primary motivation must be love, above all things. Artists must learn to share our art—and our lives—not from our neediness or our self-centeredness, but out of selfless love (1 Corinthians 13).

Discussion Questions

Note: The discussion questions in this chapter, if used in a group setting, can be unsettling and complicated, and may take some time to go through. I encourage you to take your time with this, even to the point of covering the questions in several sessions, if needed.

1. Are you personally involved in a community of faith? Is it one where you feel accepted and encouraged as an artist?
2. What kind of artist are you (e.g., musician, dancer, painter)? In that role, is there a place in your church or community of faith to express yourself? Why or why not?
3. Do you have relationships in your life where you can share your fears, failures, sins, trials, and aspirations? If so, describe them. If not, why not? Would you like one?

Frankly, the next few questions are difficult ones, not only to answer but to ask as well, because they require a great deal of self-awareness and transparency on the part of the artist. You must know yourself beyond your own self-deceptions (which by definition is hard to do), as well as be willing to share them with others.

4. Do you deal with pride or envy or struggle with some element of self-centeredness or neediness? (Hint: If you said no, guess again.) How does it manifest itself? Describe a recent instance where you had to deal with this in yourself.

5. Do you ever do things or say things in order to make people think a certain way about you (or to make people not think a certain way about you)? Give examples.

6. Does your self-image (i.e., the way you see yourself) seem to be consistent with the way people see you? Why or why not? Do you ever feel misunderstood as a result? Have you ever considered the idea that the way people see you has elements that are closer to reality than the way you see yourself?

7. Do you truly feel that you can be yourself at your church and be accepted that way, or do you feel unspoken pressures to act a certain way? If so, where do those pressures come from (e.g., internally or externally)?

Chapter 4

ART *and the* SPIRITUAL DISCIPLINES

HOW DO YOU GET TO CARNEGIE HALL?

There's no getting around it. Learning to play the piano is hard. The narrative of my life is punctuated with countless hours sitting on a piano bench learning the *craft* of the piano. I have an amalgamated childhood memory of me looking out the window, watching my brothers play in the front yard, while I stayed inside to practice. I've played my scales and finger exercises religiously since I was five, rehearsed a million songs, performed thousands of gigs, played billions of notes. And then there are the untold hours thinking of and listening to and studying this very special thing called music.

People will often come up to me after a performance and compliment me on my playing (which I always graciously appreciate). But what they don't know is that I have paid a considerable price for the ability to play the piano the way I do. Not just the hours of practice. Not just the hours spent and physical exertion expended and money paid. I've also had to listen to myself struggle with difficult passages and play a gazillion clunkers and get it *wrong* thousands and thousands of times. And I hate hearing the mistakes. It's brutal.

Occasionally, people will ask me how I make playing the piano seem so effortless. My typical reply is that there are just so many mistakes a person makes in one's musical life, and I've made most of those mistakes already, when no one was listening. So when I play publicly, most all of the notes are right ones.

It's like any discipline. People are amazed when Tiger Woods drains a twenty-foot birdie putt in the final round of a Grand Slam tournament. But the reality is, he's made that putt hundreds of times—maybe even thousands of times—on the practice green over the course of his life. So when the opportunity for a birdie presents itself, he is ready. The same devotion to skill and competency goes for performing brain surgery, flying a commercial airplane, cooking a gourmet meal, and landing a triple axel. Anything done skillfully has been accompanied by hours and hours of disciplined rehearsal.

How do you get to Carnegie Hall? Practice, practice.

This is the concept behind the spiritual disciplines. Spiritual disciplines were conceived by the early Christ-followers as a means of training themselves, over the course of their lifetimes, toward increasing Christlikeness. At the heart of the spiritual disciplines is the belief that an activity or activities practiced with discipline by an individual over a long period of time can be a catalyst for intrinsic spiritual change in that individual. In other words, they are external behaviors that aid in internal transformation. The classical spiritual disciplines include prayer, silence, solitude, meditation, fasting, study, service, the observance of holy days, and others.

And here's the thing. All of these behaviors were practiced by Jesus in His life. In fact, it was His *way* of life.

Jesus was holy by nature; that is, He was fully God. But He was also holy by practice, being fully man, because He disciplined Himself with regular fasting, with studying the Scriptures, with solitude and silence, with being in constant fellowship with His heavenly Father.

In short, He lived a lifestyle that kept Him spiritually attuned and physically ready and emotionally strong for the calling His Father had for Him.

Dallas Willard encourages us in his book *The Spirit of the Disciplines*: "If we wish to follow Christ—and to walk in the easy yoke with him—we will have to accept his overall way of life as our way of life totally. Then, and only then, we may reasonably expect to know by experience how easy is the yoke and how light the burden."[1]

Now, a disclaimer. The spiritual disciplines should not be confused with meritorious works, a belief that asserts that being good will get you to heaven or that doing some sort of penance will make up for one's sins. This misunderstanding is one of the reasons why the disciplines are neglected in evangelicalism, with its "grace alone" theology. But spiritual disciplines are not a means toward heaven. They are a means toward spiritual growth.

And to me, there seems to be a *rightness* to this method. American Christianity, like American thought in general, often treats faith as something that you add to your life, as opposed to being something that permeates every aspect of it. It's easy to segment our lives into parts: my work life, my home life, my church life. So it is equally easy to ascribe different value systems to these segments. And so people can justify having different ethical codes, different value systems, at work and at home and at church. People will treat their spouses in ways they would never treat their coworkers, or smile at a guy at church that they would just as easily flip off on the freeway. Weird.

American Christianity is defined—consciously or subconsciously —in many ways these days: as a set of rules and behaviors (legalism); as a means of going to heaven and avoiding hell (salvation); and even as a subculture, complete with its own music, celebrities, books, and television (sectarianism). And defining the Christian faith in these ways allows people to simply add it onto the belief system and the lifestyle they already have. They don't see it as one aspect of a greater whole. It is like the woman who wants to sing on *American Idol* without having ever had a voice lesson, or the man who "accepts Jesus as his Lord" but doesn't actually think it will cost him his life. Being a professional vocalist is a serious life endeavor. And so is faith. But all too often, faith becomes an accessory to the wardrobe of one's lifestyle.

But the Christian faith isn't supposed to be an add-on to your life. The Christian faith is supposed to be a *way* of life.

Because the point of Christianity is not to act a certain way and do certain things (legalism), or to have "prayed the prayer" and thus have spiritual fire insurance (salvation), or even to live within a particular cultural context, listening to Christian radio, reading Christian books, and immersing oneself in church activities (sectarianism). The point is to become transformed into Christlikeness, and in doing so, to glorify Him. And to do that, in the true historical manner of a disciple, is to live in the way that He lived.

Consider the time-honored system of apprenticeship, practiced by artisans over the centuries. A novice apprentice would be assigned menial labor, simply being in the presence of the master. As maturity set in, the apprentice would be given more complex tasks and projects, as the master would teach the apprentice increasingly difficult techniques and methods. Over time, the apprentice mastered the craft, and in essence "became the master," and it would then be his role to not only practice the craft, but to teach and model the craft to others, to pass it on to the next generation of apprentices. The apprentice is not just a student who is taught knowledge and skill. On a more profound level, he is invited into a lifestyle that produced the artistry and sensibility of the master.

This is what Jesus did. He did not conduct workshops or seminars with His disciples. Instead, He invited others to live the Greater Life, then invited them to join Him in living as He did. To accompany Him in retreat, to experience Him in silence, to pray with Him, to forsake food with Him, to serve alongside Him. And so the spiritual disciplines—the acts of solitude and silence and prayer and fasting and service—mirror Jesus' life in the same way as that of the disciples and the ancient church fathers. They provide a means by which God comes to the forefront of our lives, and we can be more fully spiritually transformed.

I really love to play the piano. But I could not have experienced the depth of enjoyment I have from playing it without having paid the price of learning the craft. For joy comes from the knowing. And in the same way, we miss out on experiencing the depth of joy of knowing God without learning the way of Jesus.

Why do so many Christian recording artists fall to sin? Why do they become involved in drugs or alcohol or extramarital relationships? Maybe it is because fame is a completely different lifestyle than anonymity. And when they lived in anonymity, before all the fame and all the privilege and opportunity that go with it, they did not discipline themselves to turn away from drugs and alcohol and sex. They had not taken the time to form a heart that loves what God loves and rejects what God rejects. Unlike Tiger Woods, they had not put the time in at the practice green learning how to sink the twenty-foot putts, or in the sand traps learning how to put the right touch on a wedge. So when the opportunities for drugs or sex came, they didn't have the strength of character to say no.

And as we have mentioned previously, we as artists seem to feel more deeply than most. Our summers seem sunnier, our winters seem colder, our highs higher, our lows lower. And our susceptibility to pleasure and fame and temptation seems higher. That is why we have such a need for spiritual discipline and grounding.

The calling of the artist includes the universal calling of humanity —to know God and enjoy Him forever. So there is much to gain for the artist by embracing the spiritual disciplines. For we, more than others, should understand that transformation doesn't occur simply by deciding to transform. We must yield to the Spirit over a dedicated period of time. We must live in the way that we purpose. We must practice, practice.

ARTISTRY AS A SPIRITUAL DISCIPLINE

A hooded monk stands hunched over his table, the smell of exotic inks wafting throughout the room. It is a cold morning, and the misty fog that wisps outside is mimicked with every breath he takes. He pulls the parchment from the box, smoothes it flat, and examines it in the candlelight. Subconsciously, he warms his fingers over the flame, as if to prepare them for the long day ahead. On the page is the Thirty-third Psalm, a piece commissioned by an anonymous royal of the court. He sees no hypocrisy in this commission, for the scriptorium was a source of revenue for his poor monastery.

He prepares a new nib, scraping it gently against his scribe stone until it shows the precise angle and tip. He has done this a thousand times and will do it a thousand more. But this is not tedium for him. He embraces the holiness of the moment, says a prayer of thanks for the privilege of this sacred act, and then dips his pen in the ink.

He understands the privilege of education. He is the first in his family to read and write, to know Latin, the language of knowledge, and he does not take it lightly. He also understands the privilege of having been apprenticed, having been trained for many years under the master scribe. As with generations before him, he began as a scribe, and through the years of devotion to the craft, he had attained the position of rubricator, assigned the exquisite task of creating ornations, rubrics, and other flourishes. There are few skilled in this discipline, with its gold leaf and colored dyes and creative opportunity. He finds personal fulfillment in being able to use his artistry in illuminating God's Word.

He also understands what it is that he illuminates—the Holy Bible, the very Word of God. There is a weightiness to this privilege, knowing that he is part of

HE HAS CRAFTED MY HEART OVER TIME, USING MY MUSIC AS A DISCIPLINE FOR CHANGE.

a long line of artisans given the responsibility of keeping the sacred Word alive for the next generation. So every letter, every meticulous detail, is a worship moment, a divine appointment of inspiration, where God meets him.

In my own life, I have found that my music—and art in general—is a means by which I am drawn more closely into communion with God. I sit at the piano, place my fingers on the keys, allow myself to focus on the presence of God with me. And then I play. Improvisations of voicings both musical and spiritual, extensions on the circle of fifths, meditations on His glory. Or sometimes it is a song of praise that comes to me in the car, when I am intently listening to the music that constantly plays in my head. Or even in the more mundane, when I am doing my warm-ups before a band rehearsal.

And more so, God has formed me through the discipline of music. The discipline of worshiping while rehearsing, the discipline of centering myself on the presence of God during warm-ups, the discipline of meeting Him in worship, the discipline of songwriting and song journaling. He has crafted my heart over time, using my music as a discipline for change.

And this should make sense if one understands that to grow as artists is, in part, to increase in our Christlikeness. For we know that we are made in the image of God, the Master Artist. And I believe that our striving toward both Christlikeness and artistry is entwined in mysterious and complex ways.

Here is the point I'm trying to make: The creation and expression of art can be a spiritual discipline for the artist. For if spiritual disciplines are indeed external behaviors that aid in internal transformation in an individual, then the activities of art—which are transcendent in nature—can be, and should be, a spiritual discipline for the artist who follows Christ. The intention of the artist should be to express his faith through his art, where God meets him, molds him, uses him, draws the artist to Himself. We must yield our art to God, and allow Him to change us through it, in intentional and disciplined ways. Madeleine L'Engle states eloquently in her book *Walking on Water*: "The discipline of creation, be it to paint, compose, write, is an effort toward wholeness."[2]

For the scribe, his art brought him closer to God and molded his faith. The activities of his vocation, practiced with discipline over a long period of time, became a catalyst for intrinsic spiritual change. God's true product was not in the parchment, but in the person. And for anyone else—the dancer, the poet, the photographer, the musician—the disciplines of their art can bring them closer to God too. The artistic disciplines become spiritual disciplines for those of us who intentionally yield our art to Him.

I can't admit to understanding this all yet. Frankly, I can't point to any specific and obvious Bible verses to show that this is true. And I am by no means an expert in the spiritual disciplines, not a master of the "long obedience in the same direction." But I know that God has used, and continues to use, my music and my art to transform me. And I know He does this in others too.

In the Shadow of God

Nobody ever seems to tell the story of one of my favorite characters in the Old Testament: Bezalel.

Bezalel, whose name means "standing in the shadow of God," was an artist. But not just an artist—he was an extraordinary artist, the first true artist on record in the Bible. (Bezalel is also a fun name to say out loud, by the way.) Craftsman, sculptor, metalsmith, architect, even fashion designer, Bezalel was chosen by God to build the Ark of the Covenant, as well as construct the tabernacle, and everything that went in it.

In the book of Exodus, God foresees Bezalel, as He ordains him before His servant leader, Moses: "See, I have called by name Bezalel the son of Uri, the son of Hur, of the tribe of Judah; and I have filled him with the Spirit of God, in wisdom, and in understanding, and in knowledge, and in all manner of workmanship, to devise skillful works, to work in gold, and in silver, and in brass, and in cutting of stones for setting, and in carving of wood, to work in all manner of workmanship" (Exodus 31:1–5).

In chapters 36 through 39, Exodus carefully describes all the inner workings of the tabernacle: the tapestries, the framing, the Ark, the table, the lampstand, the altars, the washbasin, the courtyard, the vestments, and on and on. Under Bezalel's creative leadership, all the work was done exactly as God had commanded. It was beautiful, ornate, breathtaking, complete. And the book of Exodus ends with the Cloud of God inhabiting His sacred place.

There are three aspects of Bezalel that bear consideration. The first is that he was indwelt with the Spirit of God. In fact, he is the first person mentioned in the Bible to be "filled" with the Holy Spirit. This unique distinction does not fall on a leader or a prophet or a king, but upon an artist. So God was alive in him, and he was alive to the presence of God. And the Spirit gave him the passion to bring him to complete the task.

Second, God specifically endowed Bezalel with his talents and his intelligence. He was given wisdom and understanding so that he would know the heart of God. He was given knowledge in several different artistic skill sets, "in all manner of workmanship," in order to know how to implement God's desires. And he was given the skill and talents to be able to design and fabricate the beauty that would please God. To "stand in the shadow of God" implies that he was given a divine awareness into God's plan and aesthetic. He knew how to please God with his art and had the ability to do so.

Third, Bezalel was chosen by God. This is an ongoing motif in the book of Exodus, that God used a people of His choosing to carry out His plans for humanity. In Bezalel's case, he is called "by name," for God knew him intimately, knew who he was and who he would become. He was called to a task that is important to God, so important that God involved Himself in the minute details of the tabernacle along with Bezalel. So He needed a very special person to carry out this task. Amongst all of God's chosen, Bezalel of Judah is called to build the Ark of the Covenant, that which held God's glory (Exodus 37:1).

What is not mentioned in this passage is the context of his situation, the story that lives between the lines. Bezalel is given this incredible, unprecedented gift of talent and skill and artistry. But he had free will. And he didn't have to give it back to God. He could have personally profited from this gift, created a successful business from his remarkable skills, charged for his time, given the glory and monetary gain to himself. And truly, this is what most artists and artisans do. For artists can be prideful and self-centered people. But he does not. Bezalel understands where his remarkable gifts come from and he stewards them wisely. He is not selfish in his giftedness, neither to God nor to His people. And he is true to his calling, performing his task to the delight of the Lord.

Think about that. He is the coolest, most happening artist in the history of the people of Israel. He has the status, the gifts, the venue, the prestige. And he gives it all back to God. He keeps his covenant, as God keeps His. Interestingly, after one final mention in chapter 38, we never hear from Bezalel again in Exodus. Instead, the focus is back upon God, upon His presence with His people. Bezalel quietly serves God with both skill and humility.

Bezalel is a model for the millennial artist who follows Christ. For in our own ways, we are each called "by name" to enter into the privilege of art. And in that calling, we have an obligation to steward the gifts that God gives us—honing them, sharing them, delighting God with them. For we all "stand in the shadow" of the Almighty, all are given a divine awareness of God's plan and aesthetic. To greater and lesser degrees, we all bear the potential of Bezalel.

MEETING GOD IN OUR ART

The question now is this: how do we as artists practically use our artistic disciplines as and with spiritual disciplines? I'll try to use myself as an example, although I admit that I am a sojourner, not an expert.

Allow me to use this book as an example. There is the art form of creative writing, the forming of ideas into words and phrases and emotion and meaning. And I have applied this art form toward the writing of this book. The ancients had another name for it: *journaling*.

Journaling is a discipline of engagement, where one tries to stay attuned to the Spirit of God by documenting one's thoughts and feelings and ponderings. The journal becomes a spiritual diary of sorts, and the goal is not necessarily to be complete or concise, but rather, to be honest and authentic before God. So for many months, I kept a journal in my quest to know God more deeply and specifically to help me form a personal theology of worship.

LIFE BECOMES THE ACCUMU-
LATION OF APPOINTMENTS,
NOT THE LIVING OUT OF
MEANINGFUL MOMENTS.

As a part of that discipline, I also incorporated the spiritual discipline of *study*, the active engagement of the written and spoken Word of God with the goal of hearing His voice. This is not necessarily a scholarly pursuit, but it does involve giving time for meditation upon the Scriptures and upon other books within which God will meet us. So I have read books, researched articles, and surfed different websites (check out the bibliography for some great reading). I have had many deep conversations with many of my wise and intuitive artist friends and associates. I have prayed and meditated on all these things. I have captured my thoughts on my trusty MacBook and wrestled with them in rewrite after rewrite. And through the activities of these spiritual disciplines over this extended period of time, I feel as if I know God's heart more and more, and He continues to change me. The discipline of an external behavior, in this case, journaling and study, aids in internal transformation.

Another area of spiritual discipline is the area of *slowing*. We live in a too-fast world, cramming life from alarm clock to alarm clock, defining our days with our Outlook calendars and BlackBerrys. Life becomes the accumulation of appointments, not the living out of meaningful moments. Slowing is kind of a modern form of *peregrinatio*, or voluntary exile, which was practiced beginning in the fifth century. Slowing is the deliberate act of unplugging from the world, a discipline of abstinence, where we create space to more fully enter into God's agenda, hear God's voice, listen to the leaves of the trees rustle and the wind sing.

Creativity is contrary to busyness. Creativity often takes time and space, where the soul can breathe and the hand can doodle and the Spirit of God can inspire. A hurried life full of obligations, demands, and "stuff" often leaves little room for inspiration and creativity. Indeed, it is counterproductive to it.

I have a friend, a professional musician and songwriter, who takes a weeklong songwriting retreat each year. He needs the time away from the phone and the gigs and the other demands of life to slow his pace, to be refreshed, to pause before God. And inspiration flows in these times. Now, not everyone can take a week off each year for the purpose of songwriting. But I know we as artists need to slow the pace of life to where we can hear God's small still voice. It is the discipline of slowing, another external behavior that aids in internal transformation.

I am a busy man, not only by vocation, but also by nature. There are always things going on in my life and in my church and in my head; that is the way I am. And with weekend services seeming to come along every three days, and four children cumulatively ten years apart, and creativity constantly bumping my cranial walls, my wife and I keep very busy. But I am also an introvert, one who gains strength and rejuvenation from "alone" time. I could not survive long in sanity without downtimes, purposeful and premeditated slowing in my life. So I try really hard to inject times of slowing on a regular basis—an hour or so every day, a day every week, and a few weeks every year.

There is a reason why inspiration is strained when hurried, why creativity needs time and space. It is because inspiration is a dialogue, and we must hear before we speak. God can more easily cultivate a heart that has learned to wait and be still. The psalmist reminds us: "I've kept my feet on the ground, I've cultivated a quiet heart. Like a baby content in its mother's arms, my soul is a baby content. Wait, Israel, for God. Wait with hope" (Psalm 131:2–3 THE MESSAGE).

What an appropriate image of what it is to be quiet before God. Anyone who has ever held a just-fed, just-burped baby has seen that kind of quiet contentedness. We artists need that in our lives.

The most obvious spiritual discipline for the artist is *worship*, which is one of my life passions. And though I will speak of worship separately and in more detail later, this much I will say now: the true artist is a worshiper. Even for those who *don't* follow Christ, I believe that it is pretty much impossible for one who has a creative spirit to not worship something. It may be someone we emulate, some goal to which we aspire, some ideology we espouse, or it might even be ourselves—but there seems to be always something. Because worship is a transcendent discipline that draws us in and captures us. We have the heart of worshipers, but those hearts aren't always aligned toward Him.

For the artist who follows Christ, we must not only worship, but live as worshipers of the Living God, creating worship moments in each day and corporate worship in each week and worship attitudes in our lives. Because if we don't, we will—consciously or subconsciously—find something besides God to worship.

One fairly unique way that I incorporate worship and *meditation* is at the piano. I will fix my thoughts on a certain attribute(s) of God, or a particular situation that I'm going through, or on God's grace. I try to center my soul with an attitude of openness and yielding. And I will close my eyes. And I play. I go wherever my fingers take me, creating in the moment, purposefully seeking transcendence. As opposed to Eastern meditation, which intends to clear one's mind of thoughts, Christian meditation intends to fill one's mind with the reality of God's presence. And the piano seems to speak for me in ways that my mouth cannot express. Sometimes in sorrow, sometimes in joy, sometimes in wonder. And God meets me at the piano with a psalm in my heart.

One final comment before you get the idea that I am some kind of expert. I am *lousy* at the spiritual disciplines. Really. I have failed many times trying to incorporate them into my life. It is by nature difficult for me to practice slowing. Every time I try fasting, I end up with a headache and a cranky spirit (the opposite of my intended goal!). And I would not have been so disciplined in my journaling and in study if I had not purposed to take on this project. But that doesn't mean I shouldn't keep trying. Being a Christian is to be a "disciple." The Bible does not make a distinction between the two. For in the Scriptures, to be a believer is to live as a disciple. Dallas Willard writes:

> The word "disciple" occurs 269 times in the New Testament. "Christian" is found three times and was first introduced to refer precisely to the disciples—in a situation where it was no longer possible to regard them as a sect of the Jews (Acts 11:26). The New Testament is a book about disciples, by disciples, and for disciples of Jesus Christ.
>
> But the point is not merely verbal. What is more important is that the kind of life we see in the earliest church is that of a special kind of person. All of the assurances and benefits offered to humankind in the gospel evidently presuppose such a life and do not make realistic sense apart from it.[3]

A number of years ago, I decided to try an experiment. If the spiritual disciplines are external behaviors that aid in internal transformation, I reasoned, then I didn't have to be limited to the traditional disciplines. I could *create* an external discipline that might change me (a totally artist "I-want-to-do-things-my-way" thing to do). So I did.

I decided that I would create the spiritual discipline of "hugging."

Now, this only makes sense if you knew me. I am not a huggy kind of guy. When someone would approach me with a hug, I would graciously but stiffly accept it, but I would suddenly break into a sweat and my entire body would petrify like a mannequin in a store window. I would give the obligatory three pats on the back and wait for the torturous moment to pass. I don't know why I was like this. Around my wife and my kids, I am an extremely touchy-feely person, and our family is characterized by lots of spontaneous hugging and wrestling and jumping on one another. But I knew that God wanted me to express love to the people around me, express it not only with my heart but with my body.

So I purposed to hug people. It became a spiritual discipline for me. It's crazy but it's true. When I saw someone I genuinely felt love for, or someone who needed a physical expression of care, I would suck it up and hug them. I started out slowly, tentatively, but gradually (and I mean over the period of more than a year!) I would work my way up to a dozen hugs on a Sunday morning. It was awkward at first, but slowly got easier, and eventually even became *natural*. And people responded in remarkable ways. I completely underestimated the significance of a hug given by me to another. It spoke grace, healing, love. It spoke intimacy, acceptance, agape. It was a redemptive act, used by the Spirit of God.

And here is the thing. I was not only ministering to people in a real and authentic way. The discipline was *changing* me, making me more like Christ, making my heart more like God. My heart became more tender, more attuned, more Christlike with each hug, as God hugged people through me.

Try the spiritual disciplines. Incorporate them into your life. Make them up if necessary. But yield to God, and see where He takes you.

THE TRANSCENDENT DIALOGUE

The family van was acting up, so I had to take it into a local mechanic for servicing. These are the moments that I feel most like an idiot. Because I know that at some point, I have to describe to the mechanic what I *think* is wrong with our vehicle. It starts out with me trying to name parts of a car engine (like the framathingy or the maniforked gasketabob) and ends up with me making car noises to full-grown adults.

Somewhere in the small talk—after the initial descriptions and the subsequent discussion about the weather, politics, and the local sports team—the subject of what I did for a living came up. Now, I'm always looking for an excuse to invite someone to church, so I replied, "I'm a worship pastor at a church here in town."

The mechanic's pencil stopped momentarily from filling out the invoice, as a blank stare glazed his face. "So," he ventured casually, "what is it that you do anyway?"

And in that split second of time, there were so many things I wanted to say: I wanted to say that worship is a spiritually transcendent experience with the God of the universe. I wanted to say that worship is a privilege and a command and a labor of love. I wanted to say that worship is an expression of great spiritual depth, a response to the reality of our Great God and His majesty and deeds. I wanted to say that I have the best job in the whole world, which is to lead God's people to His throne.

And then I looked into his face and said, "Well, I do the music and stuff."

"Oh," he replied.

I share this because I realize that the world doesn't really understand what worship is. And to a smaller but significant degree, I'm not so sure that the people who inhabit our church buildings on Sunday mornings really know either. Or more specifically, what it can be. And I am so passionate about worshiping God, and the transcendental nature of that worship, and the transformational power that God has within it, sometimes I find it hard to contain myself.

Now, it isn't my intent to give you a treatise on my theology of worship, although I'm sure that will poke out here. It is more my intent to speak of worship as it relates to art, and equally important, how I have experienced worship in art.

First, some attempts at defining worship. In the Old Testament, the most frequently found Hebrew word for God is *Elohim* or one of its related forms. In the New Testament, the Greek word most frequently used for God is *Theos.* According to Dr. Bruce Leafblad, "The basic meaning of these two words is the same: an object of worship."[4] So God defines Himself to us in the Bible according to our response to Him, which is to worship Him. The very words used for God explicitly designate worship to be one of our most basic responsibilities. Now I don't fully understand that. But this much I know: God desires to be with us, as individuals and as a corporate body, within the intimate context of worship.

Try to wrap your brain around this concept. God exists in three Persons, in perfect Triunity, and thus in perfect community with Himself. The vastness of creation is the outpouring of this perfect community of Godhead, and all of creation exists as a testament to His glory. The moon and the sun, the stars in the sky, the mountains and the sea, the cherubim and seraphim, all declare the glory of God. Thus, worship, rather than an event that happens on Sunday morning, is actually an eternal interaction between the Triune God and His creation. When we gather on Sunday, God, who exists in perfect community with Himself, invites us to enter into that community. God's motivation is His eternal love for us, and our response is our love to Him. We are invited into the eternal act of worship, which was initiated and sustained by God since the beginning of time.

The implications of this truth are many. We know that worship isn't about us, but it is much less about us than we realize. It does not begin with some-thing we do, but with something God has already done. It is not just about singing or worshiping in the moment, but more about aligning ourselves in such a way that we are under God's reign and rule with our whole lives. It is not about being a part of an event, but about join-ing an act of worship that is eternal and universal and transcendent.

IN ESSENCE, WORSHIP IS EX-PRESSING OUR LOVE TO GOD.

Worship is a real and transcendent and transformational en-counter with the Living God. Garrison Keillor once said, "If you can't go to church and at least for a moment be given transcendence, if you can't pass briefly from this life into the next, then I can't see why any-one should go. Just a brief moment of transcendence causes you to come out of a church a changed person."[5]

There are many valid definitions of worship. I've heard that the word "worship" comes from the Old English word "worth-ship," meaning to ascribe worth or value. And I've heard that the Old Tes-tament word for worship means "to bow oneself down." But my fa-vorite definition of worship comes simply from the book of Matthew. "You shall love the Lord your God with all your heart, and with all your soul, and with all your mind" (Matthew 22:37 NASB). In essence, worship is expressing our love to God. And in communion with God, our conversation is a language of love and grace.

Everything that we do for God's sake can be summed up in the Great Commandment, the Golden Rule, and the Great Commission. And worship is one of the purest forms of the Great Commandment.

Worship is responding to God's love by expressing our love back to Him. I side with Leafblad when he declares, "Worship is the highest form of love."[6]

Love happens within the context of a relationship. God loves us. And we respond to that love by loving Him back. We love Him with our hearts, our emotion. For our God is an emotional God, who loves us and grieves for us and celebrates with us. And He made us in His image, to feel His love and be able to love Him back. We love Him with our souls, our spirits being prompted by the Holy Spirit, who beckons us beyond the mere bounds of this physical world and into the spiritual. It is a mystery, one revealed in heaven. And we love Him with our minds, grounded in the Word, able to understand and discern His Truth and apply it to our lives in a meaningful way.

"You shall love the Lord your God with all your heart and all your soul and all your mind." For all its simplicity, that is what worship is.

And there's more. When Jesus states this in the book of Matthew, He is really quoting a passage from the book of Deuteronomy. And that quote is this:

> Love the Lord your God with all your heart and with all your soul and with all your strength. These commandments that I give you today are to be upon your hearts. Impress them on your children. Talk about them when you sit at home and when you walk along the road, when you lie down and when you get up. Tie them as symbols on your hands and bind them on your foreheads. Write them on the doorframes of your houses and on your gates. (Deuteronomy 6:5–9)

This is the context in which to place the idea of loving God. The Hebrews took this command very seriously. We are to teach this when we stand or talk or sit or walk. We are to talk about it at home and at work. We are to teach and model this to our children. In other words, loving God is a 24/7 thing. Loving and worshiping God is a way of living. Worship isn't just an action. It is not to be limited to a particular time of day or a particular day of the week. It is a way of life. It is intended to permeate everything we do and everything we are.

Now think about that with respect to who we are as artists. Since art is an expression of ourselves, not just a part of our lives but a part of who we are, then art can—and should—be used as a means for worship. This applies not just to performance art (e.g., music, dance, drama), but to all art (e.g., painting, cooking, sculpture, film). For we are to love God when we stand or talk or sit or lie down or get up. Or paint or sculpt or dance or act or perform or cook or produce or sing.

The creation of art is a spiritual dialogue,[7] just as worship is a spiritual dialogue. God inspires us, impresses us with His universe, His deeds, and Himself. And we should respond by creating and expressing ourselves back to Him, all the while worshiping in the process.

Maybe this is the ultimate spiritual discipline for the artist: to practice the presence of God and to live in constant dialogue with the Father in our art. To love God with our art as He loves us.

• • •

Summary

This last chapter, which in itself is really a quite cursory look at the spiritual disciplines, was heavily influenced by the ideas and books of Dallas Willard, who was himself influenced by generations of Christ-followers before him. I recommend reading his material, as well as that of others who practice the spiritual disciplines. Even more so, adopt for yourself a lifestyle that is disciplined toward being more Christlike. The following is a summary of this last chapter:

* We are intended to reflect the image of our Creator, to increase in Christlikeness (Romans 12:2). One aspect of this is to grow as artists, since God is the Master Artist.

* Spiritual disciplines are external behaviors that aid in internal transformation in an individual. The external activities of art—which are transcendent in nature—can be, and should be, a spiritual discipline, one that can aid in internal transformation for the artist who follows Christ.

* The discipline of art can bring us closer to God, and can be, in itself, a spiritual discipline, one that should be encouraged, nurtured, trained, and developed. "The discipline of art . . . is an effort toward wholeness."[8]

* Since art is an expression, then art can—and should—be used as a means for worship, just as our entire lives should be an expression of worship (Romans 12:1; Deuteronomy 6:5–9). This applies not just to performance art (music, dance, drama), but to all art (writing, painting, cooking, sculpture, technical arts, film).

* We should encourage artists to further develop their art as a spiritual discipline that brings the artist, and the audience of his or her art, closer to God.

Discussion Questions

1. What art form(s) do you practice (photography, sculpture, music, writing)? What did you do to become skilled at your craft? What do you now do to maintain your level of expertise? Have you ever considered that it can be a means of growing in your faith?

2. "The artist worships God with his art. It is an act of love." How does that statement make you think differently about what you do as an artist?

3. Have you ever practiced (or do you now practice) any of the traditional spiritual disciplines (silence, solitude, meditation, fasting, study, journaling, etc.)? Why do you do it? How has it benefited you?

4. Do you believe that the practice of your craft has a spiritual component to it? Have you ever considered the idea that the act of your art can be an act of worship?

5. If you are in a discussion group, take some time to share your appreciation to God for the gift of the arts that He gave to you.

Chapter 5

The CALLING of the ARTIST

DEFINING THE ARTIST

When I was about twelve years old, my father, who loved me more than I knew, became worried for me. You see, I was so enamored by—and maybe entrenched in—classical music that it was all I ever played. I would bury myself in Chopin and Beethoven, playing these recital pieces over and over and over again. It probably drove him crazy, now that I think about it, though he never let on. His concern was not about my taste in music; it was more about my social life. You see, he thought that my love of classical music wouldn't make me very popular with other kids. Which was, of course, true.

So one day, he went to the local music store and purchased a selection of music for me, music that he thought would make me somehow more cool. And of all the music that was available, of all the great material that was popular in this Age of Aquarius, he bought me this: *The Partridge Family Songbook.*

I kid you not.

It was apparent to me, even at my young age, that Dad did this out of a caring heart. So I sat him down and explained to him in my own twelve-year-old way that my playing highbrow music didn't have anything to do with my lack of social standing. (Truth be told, my social ineptness had a lot to do with the fact that I was just a dorky nerd.) To prove my point, I sat down at the piano and over the next half hour played a medley of popular songs I had recently heard on the radio (from Beatles to Bread to Beach Boys). For as long as I can remember, I have always had this innate ability to play whatever I could hum. So this wasn't anything difficult for me.

When I was done, he quietly encouraged me to learn some Partridge Family songs (which I did to please him) and told me to keep practicing. And I went back to my classical music.

There is a bit of an irony here. The Partridge Family weren't musicians or recording artists. They weren't even a real family. They were an ensemble of actors pretending to be these bus-driving, family-loving, bubble gum–playing musicians. The show was, in a literal sense, art imitating life and, in this case, doing so badly.

And while I will admit to watching the Partridge Family as an adolescent (and maybe even having a bit of a crush on Laurie Partridge), I knew that Shirley and David and Danny weren't musicians, not really. They were just faking it. They weren't like the Beatles; they were more like the Monkees. And I didn't want to be anything like that.

Before I engage in this last chapter on the calling of the Christ-following artist, I thought it would be good to finally make an attempt at defining what an artist is. Though implied, we have traveled far in our search without actually defining the word "artist," and we wouldn't want to pretend, manufacturing identity and passion on a multi-colored bus of pretension. Our understanding of the term "artist" is as foundational as our definitions of beauty and art themselves. More so, we need this definition to push forward, in order to ask the deeper questions: What is Christian art? And what is the difference between an artist and a Christian artist?

So we return to the Internet for some more real-life opinions:

No great artist ever sees things as they really are. If he did, he would cease to be an artist.[1]

> Oscar Wilde
> Author and playwright

The highest art is always the most religious, and the greatest artist is always a devout person.[2]

> Abraham Lincoln
> American president

The artist who is not also a craftsman is no good; but, alas, most of our artists are nothing else.[3]

> Johann Wolfgang von Goethe
> German playwright and poet

The work of the artist is to lift up people's hearts and help them endure.[4]

> William Faulkner
> American Nobel Prize author

Art is a collaboration between God and the artist, and the less the artist does the better.[5]

> André Gide
> French writer

The artist is not a different kind of person, but every person is a different kind of artist.[6]

> Eric Gill
> Master wood engraver

The key to the mystery of a great artist is that for reasons unknown, he will give away his energies and his life just to make sure that one note follows another . . . and leaves us with the feeling that something is right in the world.[7]

> Leonard Bernstein
> American conductor and composer

Art is not a handicraft, it is the transmission of feeling the artist has experienced.[8]

> Leo Tolstoy
> Russian novelist and philosopher

The job of the artist is to deepen the mystery.[9]

> Francis Bacon
> English philosopher and lawyer

Certain themes coalesce in these definitions. The artist has the ability to see and interpret the world distinctly and individually. The role of the artist is to encourage, inspire, and challenge. The artist connects somehow to a spiritual dimension, and has a self-awareness that relates to and reveals the greater humanity. The artist is by nature creative, expressive, unique. To be an artist is somehow to embody all of these qualities.

Note that in all of these quotes, an artist is not primarily defined according to the medium of his or her art. In other words, an artist is not an artist simply because he paints in oils or she cooks gourmet meals or they dance well together or he cut an album. The artist is not defined according to his or her creation. More so, the artist is defined according to the way he or she perceives and interacts with the world.

Said another way, recording music or directing film or writing books or acting on stage doesn't make you an artist; rather, expressing your music or your film or the written word or drama in your own unique way because you perceive the world uniquely does. Being an artist is a state of being, a state of the soul, a way of looking at oneself and the world.

This is why the Christ-following artist has such a potentially profound role in the church and in the world. We have the creative means of expressing our faith in unique and soul-touching ways. And in the vast landscape of worldviews that make up our society, we need to express our voices.

But a few more definitions are still in order. What is a worldview? Simply put, a worldview can be defined as a set of assumptions that color our experiences and understanding of the world. It is not necessarily the same as a philosophy or a religious set of beliefs, although those necessarily play into one's worldview. It is the blending of all of these things, along with our backgrounds and experiences and other beliefs, that form our worldview. It is like looking outside through a stained glass window. Whatever you see on the other side—relationships, laws, economics, politics, culture, the homeless, even art—is tinted, interpreted, and even clouded by the "lens" of the stained glass that is your worldview.

For example, I myself have an evangelical Christian, Western American, somewhat liberally conservative, male, son-of-a-Depression-era-immigrant, twenty-first-century worldview. And everything I see and do and experience is filtered through this framework. It is how I see the world. And it affects the way I interact with the world around me.

This is important to understand because it is the operative word in our next definition: what is Christian art? It is not art that is performed or displayed in the church, although it can be. It is not something with a fish or a cross or a dove or any other Christian symbol on it. It is not something that need be overtly religious or spiritual in nature. It is not even necessarily art that is produced by a Christian. In my opinion, Christian art is art that is expressed through a wholly Christian worldview.

And this distinction can be subtle or overt. It certainly need not be forced or made formulaic. But it must affect us as artists. It must affect our art. Hilary Brand and Adrienne Chaplin contend in their essential book *Art and Soul: Signposts for Christians in the Arts*:

> *In working through the most central plot of the Bible's "grand story"—creation, fall and redemption—we have put in place the beginnings of a worldview. Through these spectacles we can begin to view and perhaps question the many assumptions that are tossed in our direction. Questioning assumptions is, of course, very much in the spirit of the post-modern age, but it is also the spirit of Christ.*[10]

We stand in the shadows of differing worldviews—a mosaic of religions, philosophies, mind-sets, and historical eras. And in one way or another, art has been an expression for all of these co-existing yet unaligned worldviews. And we also live in a broken world. Because of the fallen nature of this earthly existence, we are thrust into unintended complexity—the universe has been invaded by sin, and as a result, we have disorder, distortion, disease, dysfunction. The universe does not operate as it was intended. We as Christians share the worldview that God created the world, and in spite of the world's broken nature, He is in the business of rescuing it and redeeming it. And in one way or another, our art should be an expression of that. This is what Christian art should be, honest in the brutal and complex realities of this world but also revelatory in the redemption of it.

IN GENERAL, OUR ROLE AS ARTISTS IS TO UNIQUELY EXPRESS THE HUMAN CONDITION, WHICH IS BY DEFINITION A BROKEN ONE.

One of the encouraging trends currently emerging is the advent of talented Christ-following filmmakers in the American movie industry. Refreshingly, they are not creating a genre of their own, like "contemporary Christian film." Instead, they are taking their Christian worldview and simply trying to make great films. Now, you might call them "Christian filmmakers," but it is more important to understand that they are trying to take an active role in expressing their art with excellence and, in doing so, shaping the world around us.

THE CROSS AND ART

We have now discussed the definition of an artist, and offered a definition of Christian art, that which has a wholly Christian worldview. We have now led ourselves to the *big* question: what is the difference between an artist and a "Christian" artist? What should distinguish the artist who follows Christ from one who does not? What is it to say that you are a Christian artist anyway? These are big questions, and I respond humbly with a small answer.

We discussed previously that so much of our art comes from our brokenness, our unformedness, our soul-tortures, our struggles. For it is from our incompleteness that our driving need to express often comes. We as artists have a tendency to feel more deeply, and I believe that this also means that our wounds can also be felt more deeply. We make it our business to be in touch with the pathos and soul stirrings of our world. And we make it our business to share these feelings through the expressions of the arts.

In general, our role as artists is to uniquely express the human condition, which is by definition a broken one, marred and tainted by sin. And people are attracted to this artistic brokenness, because it is so universally relatable. (This is why we are attracted to such celebrations of brokenness as country music, rap, and emo!)

But while many artists are stuck in and, in some cases, profiting from one's brokenness, I believe that the calling of the Christ-following artist is to move from brokenness to wholeness and express that in our art. This is the story of redemption we discussed in chapter 1, the story of ourselves, the story of all creation. And we as artists have the privilege of telling that story.

I THINK THAT PEOPLE DESPERATELY WANT TO HEAR GOD'S STORY, ALTHOUGH MOST MAY NOT REALIZE IT.

This is Christ working in us. We begin in brokenness—broken in spirit, broken in our sin, in a broken relationship with God. And Jesus brings us into wholeness—to be whole in spirit, whole through restoration, and whole in our relationship with our grace-filled God. We are new creations (2 Corinthians 5:17). We are renewed day by day (2 Corinthians 4:16). We are transformed (Romans 12:2). We are sanctified through and through (1 Thessalonians 5:23). Not that we are perfect, and not that we have arrived. But as Christ-followers, our art should express the journey toward wholeness that we experience in our lives. Each of our stories is a part of the meta-narrative of God's redemption of humanity, His love of mankind.

I think that people desperately want to hear God's story, although most may not realize it. But they are looking for answers to the big questions that are a part of what makes us human. We live in a world whose canvas is seemingly filled with shades of gray. It is our job as artists to more clearly and boldly draw out the dark and light brushstrokes from that gray, through our stories.

So as artists, we have this privilege to examine and express and reveal. But for us, as Christ-followers, we can also inspire and redeem and give hope in Christ.

Let me share an additional quote from *Art and Soul: Signposts for Christians in the Arts:*

Many of us would hate to be called a "Christian artist" or be referred to as making "Christian art." Apart from sounding rather pretentious, it is hardly a major selling point to galleries or commissioning editors! But there is something which justifies these scandalous labels, even for those not doing overtly religious art. As we have already seen, worldviews pervade our life and actions in all that we do. Of course, it is possible to wear two different worldview "spectacles"— one in church and one in the studio—and a surprising number of Christians seem unconcerned at doing so. But if we do our art with any integrity, our Christian worldview will unconsciously and inescapably enter our work. We are, whether we like the label or not, "Christian artists." [11]

This last quote makes me feel a bit uncomfortable, probably because I personally don't like the label "Christian artist." I frankly shy away from labels in general, disliking the boxes that they represent. (See "Art and the Christ-Follower" in chapter 2.) But the quote resonates with me in that I believe that the message of Jesus is a scandalous one, scandalous in His claims of extravagant grace and eternal redemption. Whether we embrace the label or not, we must accept the calling associated with it. And for that, we must read on.

A PARABLE OF THE POSSIBILITY

There once lived a man, neither young nor old, but in the middle of life, at the age when one measures heavily the cost of mortality. He measured his life not by the length of the day or the coming of the seasons, but by the death of his dreams. He was—once in his lifetime—a dreamer of dreams, inspired by creation, excited by the possibility.

But those days were long past. Now, there were only artifacts of his creative power—a faded painting of him on the wall, a rusty compass on his desk (for he traveled much in his younger days), a brass trumpet carefully packed in a calfskin case that lay by the large brick fireplace. No longer did the muse visit him. No longer was there a glint in his eyes. No longer did he stare into the night sky and dream. His vocation now was more grounded, more pragmatic. He was, officially, the keeper of goats.

It was not always this way. Early as a child, he showed the promise of possibility, for the sound of this trumpet in the hands of the boy would make toes tap and people dance. All who heard him were amazed. He was proclaimed a prodigy, a wonder, a genius. They showered him with praise and sought him for his gift. It was exciting to him, to feel the power of the horn, this ability to create smiles and laughter and longing among all the people in his village.

But as he grew, the excitement turned into intoxication, and the intoxication eventually became addiction. He threw himself into his craft, disciplined himself to be the best he could be. Every day and every night, he would play his horn, learning to push the boundaries of his abilities further and further. It eventually became not just something he did, but a part of his identity. For better and for worse, he no longer saw himself as a part of the whole, but as something separate, something other, something special.

By the time of his turning, when boys become men, his frustrations had become too much for him to bear. He had determined to set out for the mainland, away from his village, away from the island entirely. There he felt he would find fulfillment and happiness, where his horn would bring him the accolades and fame he truly deserved. He sought passage on a sailing ship for the faraway big city, trumpet tucked deeply in its case, waiting to be heard by the world.

Thus began a journey of spirals. He was indeed gifted, and with the displays of his giftedness came his spiral toward fame. He toured as far as his compass would take him, seeing things and doing things he never would have done in the smaller world of his village. He played for princes and popes, for generals and presidents, for the famous and the infamous. He met painters and poets, dancers and debutantes, sages and charlatans, the hopeful and the heartless.

And this apex was the beginning of his spiral downward. For the lifestyle of fame comes with a price. There were lost days and dark nights during this turbulent time of his life, a period that he does not speak of except in moments of stark self-awareness and transparency. For the spiral took him down, down, to the depths of the worst he could be. And the lingering shame is a hard thing to shake.

But there was good that came from this time too. An awareness of himself. An awareness of what is true. A humility that is neither false nor inflated. And a longing for those who loved him. But too late. In the recesses of his heart, he had purposed to put away his horn, put away the gift. For he believed that it was his path back to the dark spiral that almost took him away. So this is where he is—back in the village, living with his artifacts and memories and goats. Living. But not truly being.

Until everything changed.

A ferry began to operate between his island and the mainland. Every weekend, the white billowed sails of the ferry would pop over the horizon, transporting people and merchandise and news from the mainland right to the island, right to his very village. Some thought it a good thing, opening up commerce and communication. Others thought it terrible, for change would occur—social and economic and moral changes—and change can be very painful. Regardless, it was progress. And progress stops for no man.

People began to travel to and fro freely. The world suddenly was at their doorstep. And the changes began. There were new ideas, new ways of doing things, new possibilities. It was exciting. But not all of it. For eventually, a trend surfaced. People began to travel away, but not travel back. One at a time, friends and neighbors would buy their tickets, pack their bags, and say their good-byes. An exodus began to erode the island of its people, its culture, its being.

For good or for bad, this too was progress. But for the man who knew the danger, it was a warning bell. Not that going to the mainland was an evil thing, but he knew the evil inherent in each of us and the temptations that the mainland extolled. And he believed that through it all, people had lost sight of what was good and real and pure of their ways, their traditions. They had lost sight of the narrative of their community. They had lost sight of their being.

The man struggled with this. His mind could rationalize and justify and minimize, but his heart would not stop the pounding in his chest. He loved his village, loved what it stood for, and loved its people. And they had loved him, through thick and thin. In his internal struggle, he began to understand. He began to see himself now not only as an individual, but as a part of this greater whole. One sunny morning, as he herded his goats to the meadow above the village, he was struck by an uncommon clarity of vision.

Quickly, he ran down to his home, abandoning the bleating of his flock. He picked up the calfskin case, carefully popped the lock, and pulled the horn to his mouth. The cold metal felt good against his lips, and he blew a large breath through the instrument, warming it up, as if to say hello. His fingers fell onto the valve keys like a wallet falls into the back pocket of an old pair of pants. The familiarity of the instrument in his hands brought waves of memories to him, and he closed his eyes as if to embrace some and reject others. Then he put the trumpet back in its case, clasped the lock, and ran back to his flock.

The grassy meadow lay on a gently sloping bluff above the village. It was not far; he could see the roofs of the buildings, hear the faint village hubbub below. Once again, he took out his horn, brought the mouthpiece to his lips, warmed the tubes, worked loose the valves. And then he began to play.

The familiar melody seemed to awaken the town to a sense of awareness it had forgotten. There were stirrings below, as his townspeople came out of their homes and shops. A crowd gathered in the town center. And still he continued to play.

He was rusty, without a doubt. But as he played, as the melody became more clear and sure, he suddenly had an awareness of the Source of his gift, the Possibility of what was once his, but had been lost and forgotten. This was unexpected. And it made him smile. And play on.

The townsfolk greeted him on the meadow. Laughing, cheering, clapping, even dancing. Little children and the old ones. Teenagers who remembered the songs as a child. Even other musicians, who brought their guitars and tambourines. Soon a party had broken out, with people bringing food and drink—pastries from the bakery, milk from the dairy, wine from the store. There was a sense of oneness, of community, as the man's trumpet retold the story of their village, the narrative of their lives together.

The man's lips ached from lack of practice. He had played seemingly for hours. But the joy was overwhelming. For he did not realize how much he missed these moments, these songs, these people. And neither did anyone else.

And then it hit him. In his life, he had made his gift, his Possibility, the basis for his identity and his worth. But that was wrong. His sudden realization was this: his identity was in the community he loved and in the Creator who made him. It was not in the gift, but in the Gift-Giver and in those with whom he shared the gift.

By the time he put his horn back in the case, he knew that this was the first step in a new journey. Another spiral upward. Soon there would be people coming fro, and not just to. Soon there would be singing and laughter every week and at every gathering. Soon the village would be alive with the sounds of life and energy and renewal. Soon the trumpet would blow again.

And for that, he thanked God.

THE TRUTH ABOUT SPIDER-MAN

One of my favorite superheroes was Spider-Man. I remember as a child tracing his figure from my brothers' comic books on the sliding glass door of our patio. I thought he was so cool in that spider costume, always striking those dramatic, contorted poses. He was more human than Superman, more normal than Batman, more angst-ridden than anyone. In short, he was more like me. As powerful and as cool as he was, Peter Parker (his true identity) was still under the authority of his aunt, still had to attend school, still had painful problems relating to girls. And to my little seven-year-old mind, the chance of being bitten by a radioactive spider seemed much more likely than being born on Krypton.

There is an overarching message in the Spider-Man story, a superhero meta-narrative, which is this: "With great power comes great responsibility." Spider-Man must do his duty, fulfill his role, and battle the forces of evil, even if it means flunking a test or losing the girl or being ridiculed by the class jock. Because there is a calling associated with his special powers, and he must take this calling seriously.

This is really a biblical concept. In chapter 25 of the gospel of Matthew, Jesus speaks of "talents" and explains that we will all be held accountable for what we do with what God gives us in this life.

In chapter 12 of the first book of Corinthians, Paul speaks of the body of Christ and says that we all have God-given roles to fulfill within the body for the common good. And Jesus Himself stated: "From everyone who has been given much, much will be demanded; and from the one who has been entrusted with much, much more will be asked" (Luke 12:48b). There is certainly truth in having responsibilities for the talents and abilities and circumstances God has bestowed upon us.

Though I've lived as an artist all of my life and as a Christ-follower for the past twenty years, the journey that led me to see these roles as intertwined has been a relatively recent one. I have come to the conclusion, however, that both roles are inseparable from my identity and purpose. I experience God through my art, glorify Him with it, see His hand upon me in process and product, and experience the benefits of living my life and art in Him. So I am convinced that, as artists who are also followers of Christ, we are endowed with unique responsibilities associated with His calling upon us. Some random thoughts on this:

The Christian artist has a responsibility to respect the power of the arts. No one doubts the power of the arts. It is because we implicitly understand that they are a means of transcendence. But the arts can be used to sell fast food and spoof reality and deliver pornography with equal skill and effectiveness as the telling of God's story in our lives.

Think about these artistic expressions: Michelangelo's *The Creation of Adam*. The Broadway musical *Les Misérables*. The architecture of the Cathedral at Notre Dame de Paris. *Messiah* by George Frideric Handel. The film *Schindler's List*. All are powerful artistic expressions that point to something beyond us, to redemption and grace and hope.

Now think about these expressions: Samuel Beckett's play *Waiting for Godot*. The film *The Last Temptation of Christ*. Edvard Munch's painting *The Scream*. Gangsta rap. We get a very different picture of life and God through these powerful yet spiritually skewed expressions.

THE ARTS CAN BE TOO EASILY MISUSED, TO COERCE, OVERPLAY, DISTORT.

It is said that today's theology is not being formed in the halls of academia; it is being formed by the Hollywood film industry. So much of what people believe about God comes to them not from church, but through art and the media. The arts can be too easily misused, to coerce, overplay, distort. The church too is often guilty of superficiality, mediocrity, propagandizing, dumbing down. We must tell our story in a compelling way, but with a healthy respect for the artistic mediums in which we tell it. We must not use it to propagandize, to sensationalize, to self-promote, to manipulate.

A number of years ago, my church decided to do a weekend message series entitled "Hot Potatoes," in which we discussed such controversial topics as homosexuality, racism, euthanasia, and abortion. We really wanted to present an honest and non-judgmental biblical view of these topics, and we used a great deal of artistic elements to help us with our messages. But we weren't prepared for the aftermath of our weekend service that explored the subject of abortion.

We thought we had done a great job of programming that service: two touching songs, a real-life testimony, some visual elements, and a message that was more about love than politics. But after the services, we did not expect the number of people coming forward needing to talk to someone. Through the arts, we had dredged up the fragmented histories of many women in the audience torn by their grief, their guilt, their stories. And we were unprepared to minister to the emotional carnage that lay before us. In retrospect, we realized that although we might have done a good job artistically that weekend, we didn't do a very good job of serving those women from the standpoint of being Jesus to them. We underestimated the power of the arts to open up the souls of these women, and we were not prepared to do the real work of ministry, to help them move forward in their journeys toward wholeness.

The Christian artist has a responsibility to steward his or her gifts with excellence. Excellence, rather than being a corporate buzzword, is really a biblical principle. God deserves excellence. In the same way that God required the unblemished lamb as a sacrifice, so should we consider our art as a sacrifice to God. We need never apologize for excellence in our art, as long as it is for the right reasons.

Nancy Beach, teaching and arts pastor at Willow Creek Community Church, defines excellence as doing the best you can with what you have. It is certainly not about perfectionism or pride or performance issues. It is about honoring God with the best you can do.

How does this manifest itself? We are called to be diligent to the *craft* of our art, be it painting or writing or singing or dancing. Diligence means practicing, studying, rehearsing, expanding, exercising, training, creating. It means going to the woodshed, working on the craftsman part of your craft. Art is a lifelong endeavor, and we must apply ourselves to that end. For art has a vocabulary and we are the words and phrases that God uses to speak to people. God wants to use us, and we must be available with expressions of excellence He can use.

I am occasionally approached by someone who wants to sing on our church worship team. Now, I take every person's potential calling seriously, so there are conversations about his or her faith journey, life situation, and musical background, and there is a musical audition as well. I am always amazed at the number of people who believe they can sing, but have never had a vocal lesson. These are well intentioned, well meaning people who love God. But I wonder if they realize that it takes maybe five years of lessons to play adequate guitar or bass, five to ten years of diligent playing of the drums, and over ten to play the piano sufficiently to be at a level where you can play on the team. They may see a calling, but they have not considered the cost of the craft.

To steward our gifts with excellence is simply to work toward the potential that God gave to us. It is an issue of the parable of the talents, manifested in our art.

The Christian artist has a responsibility to excel in both style and substance in his art. There has been much said these days regarding style versus substance. Certainly style seems to be taking priority over substance these days. This is evidenced in the role models our society holds, in the way we select our political leaders, in the proliferation of plastic surgery and glamour products and exercise equipment, in what makes it onto the bestselling book and music lists, and, sometimes, even in the way we worship on a Sunday morning.

So what is the difference between style and substance? In essence, *style* is an attribute of the intrinsic aesthetic of a thing, and as such, much of what we do as artists is embodied in the word. *Substance* is the content or essence of what is expressed, and for the Christ-follower, it is our faith and Christian worldview that is (or should be) reflected in the essence of our art. It is important to know this distinction, because I think there is a trend in Christian art (as in all art these days) toward style over substance. (For example, why do Christian bands have rock videos anyway?)

Many argue style for style's sake. This is the argument that aesthetic doesn't need a reason for being (which is actually true on some level). Others argue that style creates its own substance (or as some say, "the medium is the message"). Others simply contend that substance is overrated, even unnecessary altogether. I would argue that this last argument deliberately accepts ignorance as a value. On the other side of the debate are those who would attempt to ignore style altogether in favor of greater substance. Of course, to this I would argue that doing so would be a style of its own, albeit an unintended one. And we *are* referring to style and substance in relation to art, so ignoring style is not really an option for the artist.

In the best art, style and substance are high values that are inextricably related. I am not saying that style is substance. I am saying that substance and style should be mutually present and in high order in whatever we do. Style and substance shouldn't be opposing values; they should be complementary, concomitant, and normative.

Take Apple Computers as an example. One can argue that they have an overemphasis on style, and they do win a lot of superfluous industrial design awards with their streamlined products and slick packaging. But remember that they changed the way we use computers. They developed and popularized an operating system with a style aesthetic that also contained a powerful and substantively different way to interface with the computer. Their graphically oriented operating system was not only artistic, but functional, user-friendly, productive, intuitive, and a joy to use. People forget that prior to the popularity of the Mac, PCs were sold without a mouse and with the arcane Direct Operating System. (People also forget that Microsoft was at one time a fledgling company that created software, like Word and Excel, first for the Apple OS.) Consider how unpopular computers would be today if we still used DOS. Believe me, it was *not* a joy to use.

Here is my argument: we as Christ-following artists, especially those who write and compose and originate, must endeavor to produce art that moves the soul *and* challenges the intellect. We must create works of substance capable of standing beside the many secular worldviews and do so in an intelligent and compelling and sometimes subversive way. We must appeal to the heart and the soul and the mind.

For many of us artists, it means being well-read—picking up books and trade journals and textbooks and actually reading them. It means taking classes and attending conferences, finding mentors, and learning more deeply about our crafts and our faith. It means learning to think, and not just feel, like an artist. It means working harder and digging deeper to tell the more meaningful story, in our lyrics, our books, our paintings. It means being lifelong learners in our art and in our lives. It means upholding our responsibility to steward our artistic gifts with substance and style.

One obvious example of Christian superficiality is in the superfluity of what are called "contemporary praise choruses." Although the lyrical writing has gotten much better in recent times, there remains the often heard complaint that praise choruses lack substance. Having written a number of fluffy choruses myself, I would agree with some of this assessment. The typical argument is that hymns have greater substance, but have a tendency to be stuffy and cerebral, and that choruses, while lacking substance, have a greater appeal to the heart. In response to this debate, I offer one of my favorite hymns, "The Love of God," specifically the last verse:

Could we with ink the ocean fill,
And were the skies of parchment made,
Were every stalk on earth a quill,
And every man a scribe by trade;
To write the love of God above,
Would drain the ocean dry;
Nor could the scroll contain the whole,
Though stretched from sky to sky.

Oh, love of God, how rich and pure!
How measureless and strong!
It shall forevermore endure—
The saints' and angels' song.[12]

Couched in a haunting melody, these lyrics paint a beautiful picture of God's vast love for us, and does so with substantive truth and evocative beauty. I refuse to believe that style and substance are polar and contrary. And neither should the Christ-following artist.

The Christian artist has a responsibility to live fully in the context of both the universal church and the global community. Some Christian artists view "edification" (ministering inside the church) and "evangelism" (ministering outside) as two separate callings. This dichotomy often forces the artist to choose one or the other. Some musical artists live their art exclusively within the Christian subculture, in the name of encouraging the church. Some have so engaged into this subculture that they have become estranged from the context of the world at large. Others, who find no fit within the Christian subculture, shun it completely. Disillusioned by the institutions and the dogma, they choose to live their art outside the church.

They recognize that our culture is open to spiritual things, and the arts continue to be an influence that shapes our society. So they join the world, join the mechanisms of free enterprise and marketing. They go on tour, make music videos, have light shows, appear on talk radio. They reason that their faith can be lived out in the world without the need for the community of the church to ground them, nurture them, challenge them. And some of them, somewhere along the way, lose sight of their integrity and mission and cause.

Is this dichotomy necessary? Certainly Christ did not espouse dualism in His life. He lived one way before all men, living His faith authentically in the church and out. Expressions of our art should then be valid in either circumstance, if it is an honest expression of the Christ-follower. The calling to redemption is a universal one. So is the power of art. And our story is valid regardless of the audience. So unless it is worship music (vertical by design), I encourage artists to simply do and simply be.

Apply the biblical concept of "stewardship" to our culture. If we are to be good stewards of the global culture of which we are a part, as well as the Christian subculture that exists within it, then we must be a part of the artistic expression that molds it. We must resist the temptation to insulate one from the other or to see the two as separate and unengaged. We are a part of our culture, whether we know it or not. We must live purposefully in it.

WHY IS IT THAT THE BIBLE SPEAKS MORE HONESTLY THAN THE PEOPLE WHO BELIEVE IT?

I had mentioned previously that I once had a band called Vespers, a jazz fusion group that performed in northern California. We played about half of our gigs in Christian settings (like churches and conferences) and half in secular venues (like clubs and festivals)—and we played the same music in each setting. Once, we were playing regularly at a club in downtown Sacramento, when I was approached by a couple during a break.

"That was awesome," the man declared. "What is that last song you just played?"

"Yes, it sounded *so* familiar," his female partner added.

Our reply: "'Amazing Grace.'"

The Christian artist has a responsibility to tell the truth. Artists must risk authentic expressions of good and bad, beauty and ugliness, triumph and tragedy, obedience and sin. It is ironic that our American Christian subculture feels the ever-present need to tell the button-down, happy ending of our faith in order to win souls, but it does so at the expense of glossing over the complexity and anxiety and truthfulness of the depravity of our human condition. So much of Christian drama and music is formulas and neatly tied bows. Jeremy Begbie again: "To the Church's shame, much so-called 'Christian' art has degenerated into an inoffensive and superficial kitsch which turns a blind eye to the pain in the world."[13]

We do not risk the loose ends, the mixed emotions, the messiness of real life, the foibles of our own humanity, the political incorrectness of our faith. At best, it makes Christians look naive; at worst, insincere. In the same way that songs have both major and minor chords, we must be true to the God-given cosmos, for God designed it and created the purpose that gives it meaning.

Why is it that the Bible speaks more honestly than the people who believe it? Deep in the pages of the Old and New Testaments, there are searingly honest passages on sex, on sin, on anger toward God, on the brutality of war and the selfishness of man. The Bible is honest about such flawed characters as Moses, Peter, Paul, Jacob, Samson. God's book is relevant and compelling, in part, because it does not shy away from the realities and imperfections of life. God's Word rings true because it is true.

But telling the truth is not always easy. It is extremely hard to be honest with oneself and to truly know oneself without self-pretension. It took me many years before I was able to begin to unpack my own baggage and get in touch with my hidden motivations for music (see "Reflections of the False Self" in chapter 3). There is also the continued pressure associated with being accepted by one's peers and audience. And there is the pressure to continually hype oneself in order to be noticed. On top of all that, it is a challenge to express one's art honestly in an artistically compelling way. Pulitzer Prize–winning author Willa Sibert Cather once said, "The stupid believe that to be truthful is easy; only the artist, the great artist, knows how difficult it is."

Hilary Brand and Adrienne Chaplin agree: "To portray the world truthfully as it really is to an adult audience, the artist must learn to create a complex weave of dark and light. It means learning to use the full palette of shades, confident that in hands—that have learned their craft—they will not all merge into muddy grey."14

As Christ-following artists, we must be emotionally real, culturally relevant, consistent with our worldview, devoid of distortion or propaganda. And we must tell the truth about ourselves: that we are imperfect and flawed image bearers of Christ living in an ugly world, whose only saving grace is that we have a fearfully wonderful and loving God. There is nothing more compelling to the human soul than this.

The Christian artist has a responsibility to be true to the self. There have been a number of times in my life when I wrote music with an agenda. For example, I've written theme songs for church giving campaigns, composed and arranged music for Easter and Christmas celebrations, written soundtracks for videos, even written for weddings. But there was a certain time in my life when I deliberately wrote for the worst of all reasons: I wanted to become famous.

This was in the early eighties, and I had decided that it was time to start writing radio-ready music for "the killer demo." At the time, synthesizers played by big-haired, bouncy white guys were a big deal, so I started writing in that genre (think Tears for Fears, The Police, Thomas Dolby). There isn't anything particularly hard about writing pop music (although it is extremely hard to write *great* pop music). And truth be told, I have this uncanny knack for writing great hooks that stick in your head. The problem is, in three days, these same great hooks will stay in there and turn into nails on a chalkboard.

So I wrote a series of rather dull and uninteresting love songs featuring big analog synthesizers and a drum machine. And I started production of "the killer demo."

Months later, it still wasn't done. There was something that just didn't seem right, and as much as I wrote and rewrote the songs, I couldn't get the tracks to move me. I generally started to lose interest in song after song, and the material I tended to lean into were the songs that reflected my life, songs that were a little more oblique and less pop. So I found myself stuck. I never did finish that killer demo.

Now, I know there are professional songwriters out there who can write incredible material for various artists or events. And the good ones cannot only write with craftsmanship but with integrity as well. All I know is, I can't. I have the privilege of being able to write music because I feel like it. (In other words, I don't have to feed my family with my ability to compose, thank goodness!) Maybe then I would feel differently about it. But going back to Francis Schaeffer's quote in chapter 2, music I have

> PEOPLE APPLAUD US FOR A WELL-PERFORMED SONG, BUT NOT FOR A WELL-PERFORMED ACT OF KINDNESS.

written as a vehicle to advocate a particular message to the world doesn't have as much appeal to me as simply writing music as an expression of my feelings, convictions, emotions, and personal view of reality. In essence, I had to play what I lived and live what I played.

One last thing. We artists must remember that this important gift with which we have been entrusted is not to be exalted above spiritual gifts like mercy and hospitality and service (1 Corinthians 12). In fact, these spiritual gifts often help give our artistic gifts meaning and context. This is a difficult thing for some of us artists to understand, because people applaud us for a well-performed song, but not for a well-performed act of kindness. For the sake of our own health, we artists need to create opportunities to demonstrate service and compassion, things that are away from the limelight and applause, things that grow our souls and sense of community and keep us grounded.

We are to express our arts with humility, as servants to the universal church and to the world. In this sense, we have a role to play, as one part of the body of Christ. And as the apostle Paul so eloquently describes the body of Christ symbolic in the human body, so should we act within the context of the body, to fulfill our role in concert with and in humility to the rest of the church.

The truth about Peter Parker is that he wasn't a perfect person. He was insecure, introverted, needy, and nerdy, a boy still trying to find the man inside of himself. As Spider-Man, he struggled with the responsibilities of his giftedness, with the messiness of the truth of his life, with his superpowers, and with the dichotomy of his identity. But here is the thing that most people overlook: Peter Parker was a photographer by trade and by passion. He was an artist! He was often misunderstood, often prone to living inward, one who often saw the world differently than anyone else. But in his own imperfect way, he understood the gifts given him, and he took his responsibilities seriously—and he always seemed to save the world in the end.

And in a smaller, less dramatic way, that is our calling as well.

THE ARTIST AND THE MARKETPLACE

One episode in the life of Jesus has always bothered me, probably because it seems so unlike the picture that we typically have of Him. It is Palm Sunday, the week before Jesus is crucified, entombed, and resurrected. Fulfilling prophecy, He mounts a foal, and amid the crowds, He triumphantly approaches the city of Jerusalem. Entering the city, He encounters something that so fills Him with rage, that He stops the celebration to overturn the tables of the moneychangers.

What would cause Jesus to become so angry? What would so incur His *wrath*? The sin is commercialism, the undue profiteering from the work of God. And we seem to see it everywhere, from Christian televangelists to expensive "Christian" merchandise to the increasingly exorbitant ticket prices of Christian concerts. There are people making a lot of money out there in the name of Jesus.

Commercialism is dangerous for a great variety of reasons. It has a tendency to make money our God. It compromises the integrity of Christians, especially in the eyes of those looking for unscrupulous motives in us. It skews our motives as artists, from the desire to express art to the desire for material things. It makes us think of our art as a commodity instead of as a gift. And it makes God angry.

Commercialism is really a subset of consumerism, which is the operating philosophy of our Western culture. Consumerism is the idea that we exist in a free market, made up of entities that provide goods and services, and people who consume these goods and services. There is a Darwinian survival-of-the-fittest mentality to this, as the people who are best at providing goods and services will thrive in a free market, while those who do not provide these goods and services as well will not. Businesses succeed and businesses fail, and through this free market, the consumer is provided the best goods and services at the lowest possible cost. It is a very American thing, actually.

Now, when it comes to providing goods and services, consumerism is a really good system. But when it comes to faith, it becomes more problematic. Because an underlying assumption in consumerism is that consumers and business owners must operate in their own best self-interests, in order to best meet their needs and wants. And when we allow self-interest to guide our faith, then we make ourselves the center and God secondary.

Without realizing it, we begin to see ourselves as religious consumers, shopping for the best Christian books, music, and concerts. And we see the local church not as an expression of the body of Christ, but as a purveyor of religious goods and services. So we go "shopping" for the church that has the best programs or services, the church that meets *our* needs. We rate the worship according to how it made us feel, instead of how we made God feel. We rate the sermon according to some unspoken set of religious criteria, instead of whether God was speaking to us through it. We compare the music of other churches to our own, compare the size of other churches to our own, compare the programs and brochures and (if you are a graphic artist) even other church logos to our own. These are the sins of Christian consumerism, and as artists, we must purposely seek to avoid succumbing to them. We must never make our faith centered on us.

As artists, we are too often unknowing accomplices to this entangled web of commercialism. As an artist, there is an unspoken contract between you and your audience that goes like this: "I will compose songs or write books or paint paintings you like in order to entertain you and make you feel good in some way, and in return, you will come to my concerts and buy my CDs or books or artwork. And when I stop entertaining you, stop providing the artistic goods and services that you expect from me, then you have the right to go somewhere else. For your right to be entertained supersedes my right to express myself honestly and with integrity." I know we would never say that out loud, but it is an unspoken contract nonetheless. And this contract provides the rationale for many small but significant compromises—artistic and personal and spiritual—which may make our art less about expression and more about commercialism.

A person is an anointed worship leader and songwriter, and through his pursuit of these endeavors (and with some lucky breaks), he becomes successful, even marginally famous. He is offered a record contract, given the opportunity to tour, and sees this as God's calling upon him. At some point, he begins to favor the crowd-pleasing songs, and begins to write and sing more songs that have greater audience appeal. He hones the craft of stage presence, favors his own material during worship in order to promote his latest CDs, and learns to communicate in such a way that the songs are well received. In a sense, he becomes enamored—or maybe trapped—by his need to continue to please his growing audience. He justifies this by reasoning that it ministers to a greater number of people. And although this may be true, the unspoken reality is that somewhere along the line, he became motivated to write and sing songs that sell more albums and bring more people to his concerts. He is, by all measures, successful. God is praised, the tour goes well, and there's a new album to produce. But how much of it is still about God? It is a difficult question to answer.

It's important to understand that there is a "system" involved here. The system, both in the secular and in the Christian markets, is designed in such a way that the market—and not the quality of the art—determines which artists get rewarded. Thus, a marginal artist who is able to appeal to the masses is rewarded to greater degree than a great artist who does not.

As Christ-followers, we should have a healthy suspicion for a system that favors mass appeal over individual expression, formula over uniqueness, hype over substance, market research over artistry. To varying degrees, we should hold suspect those who live in and promote the system. We should be painfully aware of our own personal (and often hidden) motivations for art, of those areas where we may have a tendency to compromise our visions and our faith for the sake of wealth and self-promotion. And we must understand that the system's rewards—fame and fortune—aren't necessarily rewards at all. They must be understood in the context of what God thinks is important. Don't define success according to popularity or gross receipts, because these measures don't necessarily mean good art (or even right living). Sometimes, it is the complete opposite.

Consider the ancient artist Demetrius. Demetrius was a skilled silversmith who lived in Ephesus in the first century. Purportedly an artist of some renown, a leader among his peers, Demetrius was best known for creating shrines for the goddess Artemis, the Ephesian goddess of fertility (not to be confused with the Roman deity Artemis, the twin sister of Apollo). In chapter 19 of the book of Acts, Demetrius stirred up a violent riot among the artistic community, accusing the apostle Paul of pointing people away from the worship of Artemis and toward this newly birthed faith in Jesus, the Son of God. Strangely, his concern was not the widespread conversion of faith; it was the loss of business to the local shrine-making industry and the loss of income he himself was incurring.

Talk about backward thinking. Not only did Demetrius believe in false gods, not only did he oppose the One True God, not only did he propagate the belief in self-described "man-made gods" with an artistic skill that comes from God Himself—but he did all of this for the worst of all reasons: money! Here was a market-driven man, who sold out both his art and his faith. And although this is arguably an extreme case, the world is full of Demetriuses, those who create their own gods, those who see their art as a means toward fame and fortune and, by doing so, oppose God Himself.

Those of us who are church leaders play this game of commercialism too, in subtle and unspoken and perhaps unrecognized ways. Truth be told, we pay way too much attention to attendance figures, too much attention to the consumerism of our congregants, and not enough attention to the hidden pride inside us that is attached to those numbers. Watch a group of pastors interact with one another at a meeting or conference, and eventually—maybe inevitably—the subject of church attendance will come up. We would never say it, but "Who has the bigger church?" implies "Who is the most successful?" Certainly, we are interested in the souls of the people who attend our churches. But to what degree are we—in unspoken ways—motivated by the attendance and giving numbers too?

Now, please don't get me wrong. I am not saying that artists shouldn't play to big crowds or that pastors shouldn't try to grow their churches numerically—because I think we should. Nor am I saying that people should not make money from their art—on the contrary, I do believe that artistry and hard work should be properly compensated. What I am saying is that we must be aware of our sin nature, our predisposition toward greed and fame-seeking. We must understand it, fear the consequences of it, hold ourselves accountable for it.

Recently, I went to a Christian bookstore to check out the new musical artists. As I approached the store, I saw a homeless man strategically situated on the bench out front. Although he was completely ignorable (as I witnessed the number of people who casually walked by him), I felt a leading from God to engage him in conversation. Honestly, a part of me didn't want to, but I approached him anyway, asked him his name, and offered to buy him lunch at the nearby McDonald's. His motives notwithstanding, he was hungry, was having some medical problems, and claimed to need some bus fare. It cost me ten dollars and about twenty minutes to know him by name, hear his story, pray for him, and maybe be Jesus to him for a few minutes.

After we said our good-byes, I thought about my actions—and the motives behind them. It would have been very easy for me to be so enamored by my own consumerism that I would ignore the small still voice and simply spend my money on the latest worship CD, instead of sharing it with this man. But the truer reality is that the integrity of my worship to God is only as good as my ability to love others in His name. This is why Jesus links the Great Commandment, to love the Lord your God, with the Golden Rule, which is to love your neighbor as yourself (Mark 12:29–31). Consumerism has a way of twisting our view of eternal things and making our spirituality about us.

All that being said, I believe that God, in His wisdom, endows some people with wealth and fame for good and purposeful reasons. There is nothing wrong with these things per se. But they must be seen in context, as gifts we really do not deserve, as gifts that should be held loosely, and as gifts that are relatively small, compared to the unsurpassed riches of knowing Jesus Christ.

Jesus unabashedly displayed His wrath at the sight of money-changers and market sellers in His Father's house. And His wrath was a righteous one, one we should not only heed, but understand and fear.

THE CALL TO HOLINESS

When I was five years old, my older brothers took me to the neighborhood grammar school. It was a warm, lazy afternoon amid the lettuce-spotted fields of Salinas, California, in the quintessential summer of 1965, and that fall I would start kindergarten. The swings were fast and the slides were hot. And eventually, we found ourselves crowded around a massive, black cast-iron drainage grate, which lay squarely in the middle of the school's courtyard. A sudden hush fell upon us as they pointed down at it authoritatively and with deliberate seriousness. "There's a dungeon under there," my oldest brother told me. My other older brother nodded in agreement. "That's where they put little kids when they're bad."

Iron maidens and rows of spine-stretching racks from hell formed in the dark, dank, granite passages of my mind. A shiver went through me like a cold wind in September. And as my two older brothers tutored me, I began to form my first perceptions of God and life and justice and theology. Really, I believe that everyone's theology begins at this young age—what we think of God and the universe and our place in it. It is in this context that I received some very wrong ideas about God's calling to us to be holy.

The word *holy* to me implied something ethereal and unattainable, meant to describe a spiritual state of perfection or a condition of sinlessness. The word described angels and scenes on stained glass; it was certainly not a word intended for normal people like you and me. But this idea is simply not true.

Holiness is not magic. It is not a spiritual state of perfection or a condition of sinlessness that one can eventually reach. It is simply God's act of setting us apart for His glory. It is an act of God, not an act of ourselves. In other words, God calls us holy in position, through the sacrifice of His Son, Jesus. We become His holy people, simply by yielding to the Lordship of Jesus. And then God makes us holy by renewing our lives, as we yield to His will, and He turns us into the people He intends us to be.

Our calling as artists includes the greater universal calling of *all* people toward holiness—to be set apart by God for His purposes, to seek the sanctifying will of God in our lives, and to apply His will so that we might grow in Christlikeness. It supersedes and permeates our calling to be an artist, a parent, a friend, an employee, a minister.

I mentioned earlier that my spiritual maturity is characterized in part by a greater understanding of my own sinfulness, my own humanity. The flip side of that is that as I have matured, I am increasing in my understanding of God's holiness. That is a gift, you know, to be given greater insight into the nature of God, to know Him more deeply. I am learning not to take that for granted.

As I grow in my faith, I am becoming increasingly aware of my own sinfulness and God's holiness. It is a continually sobering revelation. Through my own power, I am not the person God intends me to be. I lust, envy, covet, demean, compare, dismiss. I am self-centered, self-serving, self-promoting, selfish. I know deep down that these feelings come from my own inherent insecurities, my neediness, the family-of-origin issues deeply programmed into me, and an underdeveloped understanding of myself and the world. And I hide, deny, avoid, and minimize this about myself to myself.

Too often, I make my faith about me. I become prideful about my own holiness. I become like the Pharisees. I accept the applause intended for God. I think more highly of myself than I should. I grasp at significance and pleasure and control apart from God.

But all of that being said . . .

Through God's love, I am becoming more grace-filled, loving, kind, generous, self-sacrificing. I am becoming more hopeful, positive, believing, encouraging, redemptive. I am learning to surrender more of my will, my art, my self. I am generating the fruit of the Spirit, "love, joy, peace, patience, kindness, goodness, faithfulness, gentleness and self-control" (Galatians 5:22–23), in greater measure. I am learning to walk in holiness. And in doing so, I am learning to express art that is holy. I am learning to set it apart for God's glory. If our lives are to become holy, and our art is an expression of our lives, this only makes sense.

As I learn to yield more and more of my life, I am becoming who God wants me to be. And I am liking who I am becoming.

• • •

Summary

When I was a little kid, something happened to me that would change me forever: I began to wear eyeglasses. At the tender age of nine, I began this lifelong dependency on a delicate appliance that sat on the bridge of my little nose. And this is how it happened.

Once a year, the school nurse would make the rounds to all the classes, administering vision tests with her cardboard posters of upside down, inverted, and reversed "E's." So it was no surprise when we got back from recess to see her set up in the back of the classroom. Eventually it was my turn to take the test, and as I placed the optometric spatula over my right eye, then my left, it became obvious that something was wrong. Past the first few lines, things became fuzzier and fuzzier. And I flunked the test, even with my friends trying to whisper the answers to me. My vision was getting progressively more nearsighted, although I didn't realize it. I thought that all little girls and boys had trouble seeing the blackboard.

Our family optometrist was a burly-handed man with a deep, gentle voice. He smelled faintly of Old Spice. I remember his diplomas on the wall, and the big barbershop-like chair in the middle of the room, and the space-age lens machine that clicked in dramatically increasing clarity. There was something about Dr. Beaumont—his mannerisms, his deep voice, the way he looked into my eyes and said, "Is this better? Or this?"—that would actually hypnotize me. My dad would have to lead me by the hand back to the car, I was in such a trancelike state after being fitted with my new prescription. I remember looking out the car window, amazed at the clarity, and also being so relaxed from the experience that I couldn't make a fist.

Every year, I went back to get my eyeglasses prescription updated, and every year my eyesight got worse. He prescribed my eyeglasses originally for reading, but over time, I wore them more and more often. Eventually, they became a part of me. I have worn them for decades now; I have a hard time imagining life without them.

In a way, going through this exercise, of forming this theology of art, has been like that. I feel like I have put on a new set of glasses, and I can see things with a clarity I haven't had before. My spiritual worldview seems to have better cohesiveness and order, and my purpose in life seems a little more clear. Things are more in focus. I can see the blackboard. So I am grateful for the opportunity to have gone through this study, and for the insights I have gained. And I intend to continue to be a student of the theology of art, to keep my spiritual eyeglasses prescription updated for the rest of my life. I consider it a work in progress, as I expect God will reveal more about Himself over the course of the pages and chapters of my life.

The following is a summary of our last chapter, The Calling of the Artist:

- Christian art can be defined as art that is expressed through a wholly Christian worldview, a set of assumptions that color our experience and understanding of the world. "If we do our art with any integrity, our Christian worldview will unconsciously and inescapably enter our work."
- Art often comes from our universal brokenness. However, the calling of the Christ-following artist is to move from brokenness to wholeness and express that in our art (2 Corinthians 4:16; 5:17; 1 Thessalonians 5:23). This is what differentiates the Christian artist from other artists—that we not only express our brokenness but our redemptive road toward wholeness.
- Because artists have unique gifts and talents, they also have unique responsibilities (Luke 12:48) and calling (Exodus

31:1–5). They include the responsibility to respect the power of the arts, steward our craft and use it wisely, strive toward both style and substance in our work, live fully in the context of both the universal church and the global community, tell the truth in our art, and be true to ourselves.

❧ We live in a world driven by economic forces that can cause us to compromise not only our artistic vision but our spiritual integrity as well. We must understand our own predispositions toward compromise, and push back against our susceptibility to greed and fame.

❧ Our calling as artists includes the greater universal calling of all people toward holiness—to be set apart by God for His purposes, to seek the sanctifying will of God in our lives, to comply and be in tune with the Holy Spirit, and to apply His will so that we might grow in Christlikeness and help others experience life in His Kingdom (Ephesians 4:22–24; 1 Thessalonians 4:1–8).

Discussion Questions

1. Do you consider yourself a "Christian artist"? What do you think about that label? Does your art reflect a Christian worldview? In what ways?

2. In whatever art form(s) you express, do you think you steward your craft well? How? Do you believe that you strive toward both style and substance in your work?

3. Do you express your art in the church or in the world (or both)? How do you do that? Do you differentiate between the two? If so, how?

4. The pressures of Christian consumerism are pretty pervasive. Do you experience the pressure to compromise in your art, either spiritually or artistically? If so, what specific pressures do you encounter? Which of these pressures are external and which are internal (or both)?

5. This chapter contends that the calling to art includes the greater universal calling to holiness. How does that change the way you look at your craft? How does that change the way you live your life?

6. This last chapter required some soul-searching. Do you believe that you are in touch with your personal predispositions toward sin? Do you understand your mechanisms for self-deception and justification in this area? Are there people in your life who speak truth to you?

AFTERWORD:
IMAGINE THAT

There is a part of me that wishes for another renaissance, another period of rebirth and renewal.

Imagine that art and beauty were once again universally held values. That they were valid and esteemed expressions in the church, and not just mediums for a message.

Imagine that followers of Christ lived in a normative state of mystery and grace and holiness, one so winsome and appealing to the world that it could not ignore us.

Imagine that the church played itself like a sacramental orchestra, with passages of unison, harmony, and even dissonance bathed with a corporate grace and awe—the music of our lives played out like a symphony.

Imagine that streams of artistic creativity would flow from the river of our collective expression, and art and life would be celebrated and encouraged and enjoyed.

Imagine a community of artists who love God, love the world, and express this love through their art.

And out of this renaissance would be a sense that God is an ever-creative God, inspiring and enjoying His people and His creation. This is my hope for the artist, my hope for the church, my hope for the world.

Notes

Chapter 1: God the Artist

1. Madeleine L'Engle, *Walking on Water: Reflections on Faith and Art* (Colorado Springs, CO: Shaw Books, 2001), 56.

2. Alan Jacobs, *The Narnian: The Life and Imagination of C. S. Lewis* (San Francisco: HarperOne, 2008), xxi.

3. The *Pieta* (1499) is a famous marble sculpture by Michelangelo depicting Mary holding the body of Jesus immediately after the crucifixion. It is on display in St. Peter's Basilica in Vatican City.

4. Thomas Dubay, *The Evidential Power of Beauty: Science and Theology Meet* (San Francisco: Ignatius, 1999), 193.

5. Jeremy Begbie, *Voicing Creation's Praise: Towards a Theology of the Arts* (London: T & T Clark, 1991), 205.

6. Ibid., 227.

7. L'Engle, *Walking on Water*, 80.

Chapter 2: Art and Faith

1. At the risk of showing my age, the *Kung Fu* television series ran from 1972 to 1975 and popularized the martial arts in the U.S. It was a big deal for an adolescent like me.

2. "Art," Dictionary.com, http://www.dictionary.com.

3. Ibid.

4. Ibid.

5. Ibid.

6. Ibid.

7. Ibid.

8. "Art," ThinkExist.com, http://www.thinkexist.com.

9. Ibid.

10. Ibid.

11. Ibid.

12. Ibid.

13. Ibid.

14. Ibid.

15. Ibid.

16. Ibid.

17. Ibid.

18. Ibid.

19. Ken Gire, *Windows of the Soul* (Grand Rapids, MI: Zondervan, 1996), 11–12.

20. Jeremy Begbie, *Voicing Creation's Praise: Towards a Theology of the Arts* (London: T & T Clark, 1991), 247.

21. *Sumi-e* is the art of East Asian ink and wash brush painting.

22. "Buckminster Fuller," ThinkExist.com, http://www.thinkexist.com.

23. Catherine Michaud, "The Art of Making Life Beautiful" (paper presented at Theological Insights conference, October 11, 1996).

24. Thomas Dubay, *The Evidential Power of Beauty: Science and Theology Meet* (San Francisco: Ignatius, 1999), 17.

25. Francis Schaeffer, *Art and the Bible* (Downers Grove, IL: InterVarsity, 2007), 55.

26. Ibid., 56.

27. Begbie, *Voicing Creation's Praise*, 248.

28. Henri Nouwen, *The Return of the Prodigal Son: A Story of Homecoming* (New York: Doubleday, 1994), 134.

29. Madeleine L'Engle, *Walking on Water: Reflections on Faith and Art* (Colorado Springs, CO: Shaw Books, 2001), 9.

Chapter 3: The Artist in Community

1. Ken Gire, *Windows of the Soul* (Grand Rapids, MI: Zondervan, 1996), 57.

2. Jeremy Begbie, *Voicing Creation's Praise: Towards a Theology of the Arts* (London: T & T Clark, 1991), 220.

3. David Bayles and Ted Orland, *Art & Fear: Observations on the Perils (and Rewards) of Artmaking* (Eugene, OR: Image Continuum, 2001), 45.

4. Dr. Bruce Leafblad, "Music, Worship, and the Ministry of the Church" (lecture presented in January 1978, Western Conservative Baptist Seminary).

5. Warren Bennis and Patricia Ward Biederman, *Organizing Genius: The Secrets of Creative Collaboration* (New York: Addison-Wesley, 1997), 5.

6. When I say, "the modern American Christian subculture," I refer to that which was

birthed through the Jesus movement of the early 1970s. When I became a Christ-follower in 1985, this movement had become more sophisticated (commercially and otherwise), but was nonetheless in its "adolescence," with Amy Grant and Michael W. Smith replacing pioneers such as Lovesong and Randy Stonehill. There was great music coming out of this time, but not a lot of it.

7. Gire, *Windows of the Soul*, 20.

8. In Isaiah 6:1–8, the prophet's first thought upon seeing the Lord God upon His throne was to acknowledge his own sinfulness. True humility is knowing our place before God, and that is where worshippers should begin when we come before the throne.

9. Quoted in Gire, *Windows of the Soul*, 189.

Chapter 4: Art and the Spiritual Disciplines

1. Dallas Willard, *The Spirit of the Disciplines: Understanding How God Changes Lives* (San Francisco: HarperCollins, 1988), 8.

2. Madeleine L'Engle, *Walking on Water: Reflections on Faith and Art* (Colorado Springs, CO: Shaw Books, 2001), 74.

3. Dallas Willard, *The Great Omission: Rediscovering Jesus' Essential Teachings on Discipleship* (San Francisco: HarperOne, 2006), 4.

4. Dr. Bruce Leafblad, "Music, Worship, and the Ministry of the Church" (lecture presented in January 1978, Western Conservative Baptist Seminary).

5. Quoted in Ken Gire, *Windows of the Soul* (Grand Rapids, MI: Zondervan, 1996), 120.

6. Leafblad, "Music, Worship, and the Ministry of the Church."

7. Jeremy Begbie, *Voicing Creation's Praise: Towards a Theology of the Arts* (London: T & T Clark, 1991), 220.

8. L'Engle, *Walking on Water*, 74.

Chapter 5: The Calling of the Artist

1. "Artist," ThinkExist.com, http://www.thinkexist.com.

2. Ibid.

3. Ibid.

4. Ibid.

5. Ibid.

6. Ibid.

7. Ibid.

8. Ibid.

9. Ibid.

10. Hilary Brand and Adrienne Chaplin, *Art and Soul: Signposts for Christians in the Arts* (Downers Grove, IL: InterVarsity, 2001), 67.

11. Ibid., 185.

12. "The Love of God" (1917), written by Frederick M. Lehman, public domain.

13. Jeremy Begbie, *Voicing Creation's Praise: Towards a Theology of the Arts* (London: T & T Clark, 1991), 213.

14. Brand and Chaplin, *Art and Soul*, 55.

BIBLIOGRAPHY: ROAD MAPS ON THE JOURNEY

BOOKS

Walking on Water: Reflections on Faith and Art
  Madeleine L'Engle
  Shaw Books, 2001

The Evidential Power of Beauty: Science and Theology Meet
  Thomas Dubay, S.M.
  Ignatius Press, 1999

Voicing Creation's Praise: Towards a Theology of the Arts
  Jeremy S. Begbie
  T & T Clark, 1991

Windows of the Soul
  Ken Gire
  Zondervan, 1996

Art and the Bible
  Francis Schaeffer
  InterVarsity Press, 2007

The Return of the Prodigal Son: A Story of Homecoming
> Henri J. M. Nouwen
> Doubleday, 1994

The Spirit of the Disciplines: Understanding How God Changes Lives
> Dallas Willard
> HarperCollins, 1988

The Great Omission: Rediscovering Jesus' Essential Teachings on Discipleship
> Dallas Willard
> HarperOne, 2006

The Heart of the Artist
> Rory Noland
> Zondervan, 1999

The Narnian: The Life and Imagination of C. S. Lewis
> Alan Jacobs
> HarperOne, 2008

Art and Soul: Signposts for Christians in the Arts
> Hilary Brand and Adrienne Chaplin
> InterVarsity Press, 2001

Organizing Genius: The Secrets of Creative Collaboration
> Warren Bennis and Patricia Ward Biederman
> Addison-Wesley, 1997

Modern Art and the Death of a Culture
> H. R. Rookmaaker
> Crossway Books, 1994

An Hour on Sunday: Creating Moments of Transformation and Wonder
Nancy Beach
Zondervan, 2004

PAPERS

"The Art of Making Life Beautiful"
Catherine Michaud, CSJ
Paper presented at Theological Insights conference,
October 11, 1996

"Music, Worship, and the Ministry of the Church"
Dr. Bruce Leafblad
Lectureship presented in January 1978 at
Western Conservative Baptist Seminary

"Redeeming the Arts: An Issue Paper"
Colin Harbinson, Mary Jones, David Potvin
Forum 2004
The Lausanne Committee for World Evangelization
Pattaya, Thailand

WEBSITES

www.dictionary.reference.com
www.thinkexist.com
www.quoteworld.org
www.vangoghgallery.com
www.preservationhall.com
www.bobkilpatrick.com
www.crosswalk.com
www.christdesert.org/noframes/script/history.html

www.imago-arts.on.ca/lausanne/cover.htm

www.biblegateway.com

http:/artsandfaith.com/t100/

For More Information

The author invites all artists who have read this book to send their comments, experiences, and insights to him through his website at www.manuelluz.com.